The Making of a Civil Rights Leader José Angel Gutiérrez

José Angel Gutiérrez

PIÑATA BOOKS

Arte Público Press
Houston, Texas

This volume is made possible through grants from the Charles Stewart Mott Foundation, the Ewing Marion Kauffman Foundation, the Rockefeller Foundation, and in part by the City of Houston through The Cultural Arts Council of Houston/Harris County.

Piñata Books are full of surprises!

Arte Público Press
University of Houston
452 Cullen Performance Hall
Houston, Texas 77204-2004

Cover design by James F. Brisson
Photos courtesy of José Angel Gutiérrez

Gutiérrez, José Angel.
    The Making of a Civil Rights Leader / José Angel Gutiérrez.
        p.   cm.

    ISBN-10: 1-55885-451-7 (alk. paper)
    ISBN-13: 978-1-55885-451-2
1. Gutiérrez, José Angel. 2. Gutiérrez, José Angel—Childhood and youth. 3. Gutiérrez, José Angel—Family. 4. Mexican Americans—Texas—Crystal City—Biography. 5. Civil rights workers—Texas—Crystal City—Biography. 6. Political activists—Texas—Crystal City—Biography. 7. Mexican Americans—Civil rights—History—20th century. 8. Mexican Americans—Civil rights—Texas—Crystal City—History—20th century. 9. Crystal City (Tex.)—Ethnic relations. 10. Crystal City (Tex.)—Biography.   I. Title.
F394.C83G89 2005
976.4'437063'092—dc22   2004060014
[B]   CIP

♾ The paper used in this publication meets the requirements of the American National Standard for Information Sciences—Permanence of Paper for Printed Library Materials, ANSI Z39.48-1984.

5 6 7 8 9 0 1 2 3 4   10 9 8 7 6 5 4 3 2 1

Table of Contents

This book is dedicated to Norma Williams, a Chicana from Kingsville, Texas. She inspired me to write this book so that younger generations would know about my civil rights struggles. My struggles were like hers, except she labored primarily in higher education, seeking excellence in scholarship. And to my first grandson, Juan Marcel Tijerina, from my daughter Tozi Aide Gutiérrez, so that he can learn about his "kranpa."

Acknowledgments

My parents, Angel Gutiérrez Crespo and Concepción Fuentes Casas, provided a wonderful home and family environment for me. I was an only child, so I grew up with the most positive role models and nurturing parents. They made me the focus and central part of their lives. I received the best from each of them.

In my barrio of *México Grande* in *Cristal*, as the Chicano community called Crystal City, Texas, I had many friends, *camaradas*. El Junior (Pete Galván, Jr.), Chibeto (Gilbert Martínez), Pichón (Rudy Palomo), Panchillo (Francisco Rodríguez), Cuco (Refugio Sandoval), and I were the best of friends. I was called *bebito* when I was a child, then Angelito, and later on in high school El Diablo. Once I reached junior high and high school, the circle of friends widened to include guys from other parts of our barrio and other barrios in town. Gepo (Gáspar Méndez), Lalillo (Lalo Martínez), and Chale (Charles de la Rosa) were from my barrio, just further away than West Edwards Street, my street. Bocho (Ambrosio Meléndrez), Chevo (Eusebio Guerra), and El Jerry (Jerry Perales) were from the swimming pool area. El Diablo (Joe de Hoyas), *El* Chicken Eye (Ezequiel Romero), and La Tripa (Rafael Tovar, Jr.) were from the Avíspero barrio. Ruflas (Raúl Trejo) and La Pepina (José Villarreal Jr.) were from *México Chico*.

I had many friends who were girls, but the culture at the time did not permit you to hang out with them as much as with the boys. Chagua Vargas was my across-the-street neighbor and baby sitter. Berta Mojica, Dora and Carmen Palomo, Mary and Minerva Tamez, Olga Mena, Olga Martínez, Olga Tovar, Ofelia Perales, Gloria de la Cruz, Lupe Hernández, Raquel Estrada, Frances "Pancha" Ramírez, Francis and Nellie Benavides, Noelia and Betty Martínez, Irma Serna, Linda Juárez, Isabel Calderón, Anna Rojas, Noemi Palacios, and Rosa Jilpas. Some Anglo girls befriended me: Shirley Guyler,

Joyce Cook, Sylvia Bookout, Brenda Ray, Patricia Gregory, Janet Coker, Gladys and Lois Crawford, Lynn Pegues, and Johnnie Chris Speer. Anglo girls at that time could not become your girlfriend, their parents would not allow it.

Then I had buddies in college who helped me to develop, as did my *camaradas* in the barrios of my hometown. And I went to several colleges. At Uvalde's Southwest Texas Junior College, I remember Gabe Tafolla (Uvalde), Greg Gutiérrez (Asherton), and Juan Patlán (Carrizo Springs). At Texas A&I Kingsville, I met my first wife, Luz Bazán (Falfurrias), as well as *los camaradas* Carlos Guerra (Robstown), Lilian Tobín (Palito Blanco), Lydia Zárate (Falfurrias), Gilbert Anzaldúa (Harlingen), Efraín Fernández (Kingsville), and Alberto Huerta (Corpus Christi). I also met Anglos who became my best friends, such as Bill Richey (Harlingen), Pat Lawrence (Houston), Braden Rawlins, Fred Cuny, and James Belt (Harlingen) who was black. While at the various colleges, I met many other students, teachers, neighbors, and people in the communities who are too numerous to mention, all of whom also had an impact on my life.

I also wish to acknowledge and thank Rosalie Robertson and Bill Andrews who worked with the University of Wisconsin Press when a book on my political history was published. Henry A.J. Ramos and Nicolás Kanellos are helping me see this project to fruition. Nick tirelessly corrects my writing to make it readable. I want to thank the entire staff at Arte Público Press, particularly Marina Tristán and Mónica Parle. I e-mail Marina more frequently than anybody else about my books and related questions. Mónica does a great job with marketing and helps with my travel for book signings across the country.

And as you would expect, I acknowledge the role my family plays in my book writing. They have been and continue to be endlessly patient with my absences, while I go to write or think or dictate my thoughts. Gloria, my wife, Andrea and Clavel always forgive me for not going with them to their important activities, more often than not, as did Adrian, Tozi, Olin, Avina, and Lina when they also were at home. They usually read portions of my drafts of chapters. Thank them for what you now have in your hands.

Introduction

Every one of us has a unique, dramatic story to tell. We often tell that story in oral fragments during conversations and during arguments with others. Seldom do we write about ourselves. We should. If we do not write about ourselves, who will? I wrote this book to reach a young audience who can learn from my life experiences. I want you to know how to change the world. I tried and I did, somewhat. An unfinished job remains for you and me together to continue. In many, many ways, my life story is much like that of any other child of Mexican parents growing up in the United States. I learned to be a Mexican at home with my parents until I reached public-school age. Then, I was forced to forget Spanish and learn English, at least while in school. We do spend more time in school with others than with family or friends in the neighborhood.

In school, every time I was caught speaking Spanish I was paddled or given the option of a three-day suspension. If I took the suspension, I had to play hooky because if I showed up at home, I'd get paddled there. I learned to hate everything about Spanish, including those who spoke Spanish, beginning with me. I had to fake being anything but Mexican at school. I had to become three people in one: Mexican at home, Anglo while at school, and Chicano in the barrio. Trying to be Anglo in school to please teachers made my classmates angry. If I answered a question correctly or raised my hand with an answer, some *bato* or *ruca* (guy or gal) in the back would sneer, "*¿Te crees muy grande?*" (You think you're a big shot?) or "*¿Quieres ser gabacho?*" (You want to be white?) It seemed as if my Mexican classmates were saying that if you were smart, fast, informed, bold, and earned A's in course grades, you were trying to be Anglo. That attitude, to me, meant that being Mexican was to be dumb, stupid, slow, negative, and to drop out of school. I decided not to dumb down for anyone. I went for excellence. I wanted to be better than the Anglos. And in many respects, I was. I never saw myself as a victim and I never let myself become a victim.

From time to time, I was made a victim and learned to experience *coraje*, rage. But I learned not to let rage, much less hate, consume me. I learned to channel those strong energies into productive endeavors and positive attitudes. I learned to say "*Yo nací bien, pregúntale a mi mamá.*" (I am well born, just ask my mother.) What mother does not tell her child that she or he is the best? Adversity, tragedy, bad times, defeat, and loss became my friends. I made those occurrences become my windows of opportunity. While others saw an end, I saw a beginning. When others felt like despair and nihilism, I reached for the stars and soared with optimism. My constant reaching and overreaching with my mind developed in me the ability to envision the future. I always see the forest and the individual trees at the same time. I see the universe and the stars at the same time. Most everybody else I know can only do this when watching a movie or television show. Ever wonder why you can see that whole screen and the individuals or events at the same time? Ever wonder why you can hear a song with lyrics and hear it all at the same time together with the various instruments? Have you figured out why some people can process faster than you? I call this connecting the dots. To get to envisioning or connecting the dots or seeing the big picture, the forest, the universe, all you have to do is practice imagination. Go from the known to the unknown. Embrace uncertainty. Take calculated risks. March out of step. Think the unthinkable. Make your hopes, wishes, and dreams real.

During the 1993 U.S. Senate Special Election in Texas, I ran for a senate seat. In one of my few radio commercials and in almost every speech, I would ask: "If not now, when? If not me, which of you?"

My generation lived during an era in which Mexicans were governed. Your generation lives in an era when Mexicans will govern. I ask you now: Are you prepared to lead and govern? If not now, when? If not you, then who?

The Three Me's

There are three me's: me, myself, and I. What do I mean by that? My father, Angel Gutiérrez Crespo, was a Mexican born in Matamoros, Tamaulipas, Mexico and raised in Torreón, Coahuila, Mexico. While in Torreón, he studied medicine, hoping to become a doctor. This was during the Mexican Revolution of 1910. General Francisco "Pancho" Villa* attacked and took control of Torreón the first time around in 1917. Villa conscripted every one of the young medical students from Torreón into his revolutionary army. He made them his medical corps. Villa would load his troops and horses into railroad cars and ride all night into the interior of Mexico, attack, then load all the injured, maimed, dead horses and men, and return north, usually to Chihuahua. The medical students had to care for the wounded men and animals during the train ride back. Those attacked by Villa never knew how badly they had hurt his army because they had no body or animal count. And Villa's medical corps worked feverishly on the injured and wounded, and managed to save many lives of both men and horses. My dad had a great on-the-job training experience. During the second takeover of Torreón, Villa left my dad in charge of the civilian population, and then Villa quit fighting and retired to Parral, Chihuahua. My dad was then elected mayor of Torreón in 1929. But he did not get along with another military man, Plutarco Elías Calles, who wanted to become the president of Mexico. My dad left Mexico for the Rio Grande Valley in the United States and ended up in Crystal City, Texas, where he set up his medical practice and met my grandfather, Ignacio Fuentes. They became buddies. My grandfa-

---

*His real name was Doroteo Arango.

1

ther had a large family. My mother, Concepción, was the oldest child, and my father fell in love with her at first sight. The problem was that my dad was fifty-two-years old then, and my mom was only sixteen. As was the custom back then, the two grown men cut a deal without consulting my mother or asking her wishes. My grandfather agreed to let my father marry my mother, if he also agreed to take care of her family, should something happen to him later in life. My dad agreed, but my mother did not. They were married against her will, anyway. It took ten years from when they married for me to be born on October 25, 1944.

When my father first came to the United States, he did not come with the idea of staying. He was going to go back to Mexico as soon as his political fights with Calles had ended, but they never did. They got worse because Calles became president of Mexico. My father went back from time to time because his mother, Marcelina, still lived in Torreón, as did his son, Horacio, from another woman. He had married my mom and taken her to Torreón, but she did not like it there, and my grandfather had died in the race riots in the mid 1940s while working in Detroit, Michigan. My father had promised to take care of the Fuentes family, so he had to stay in Crystal City from then on. But, in his mind, my dad wanted to recreate his Mexican world here in Crystal City, Texas, in the United States. His politics were Mexican politics. He didn't look to Austin, Texas, or Washington, D.C. for what was important in his life. He looked to Torreón and Mexico City. The newspapers he read were the Mexican newspapers. In fact, I remember him subscribing to Torreón's daily newspaper, *La Opinión*. It arrived by mail, sometimes three or four at a time. He also bought other Mexican newsmagazines, *Mañana, Siempre,* and *Policía,* from the local vendor, Juan Ruiz. Those were magazines he made me read before he placed them in his waiting room for patients. When we would go to Piedras Negras, Coahuila, across from Eagle Pass, Texas, he would buy a bunch of magazines, newspapers, and books *en español*. At home, we used to listen to the Mexican radio at night. His favorite thing was to make me listen to Crí-crí, *el grillito cantor,* a kid's program about a singing cricket. That was his way of helping me with Spanish. He insisted that I learn Spanish and he saw to it that I did. He would make me read and discuss with him *en español* the radio program and the news. We would also sit outside in the backyard almost nightly and look at the stars while my mother would water her plants, trees, and the grass. We had lots of trees—pecan, regular orange and tangerine and lemon, grapefruit, peaches, plums, and palms—in our large backyard. He would talk to me and mother about current events. He would tell me about astronomy and the constellations and also Aztec and Greek mythology. He would also narrate short stories from the classic literature, all in Spanish. And I would have to repeat and explain to him *en español* what he had just told me. That was his way of making sure I listened, understood, comprehended, and recalled, like quizzing me on the spot. He wanted me to grow up to be a Mexican. He had no use for English, didn't think it was necessary. I realize now that he was reacting to the prejudice and the problems that he had run into with English-speaking professionals. He didn't have hospital privileges, even though he was a doctor in Crystal City. Some of the Anglo growers and ranchers would leave their injured Mexican workers right there on our doorstep. Just leave them. They made no arrangements about who was going to pay for treatment, medicine, or consultation, nothing. A few times I also saw the police bring injured prisoners for my dad to treat. The police claimed they had hurt themselves or some other Mexican had hurt them. But that was not what they would say to my father when the policeman was not around. These Anglos acted as if it was Dr. Gutiérrez's responsibility; he was a Mexican doctor, so he should take care of his own.

We would make frequent trips to Mexico. I was born in Crystal City but baptized in Torreón. My father wanted me to have Mexican *padrinos,* godparents. They were Agustín and María Ester Gurza from Torreón. They later moved to San José, California, and a couple of times Agustín invited my dad to relocate and practice with him, but it didn't work out. My dad kept his bank accounts in

Piedras Negras, Mexico. He kept his Mexican citizenship. He wanted to die in Mexico. He wanted to be buried in Mexico. That was his dying-breath request, "Bury me in Mexico."

I'm sure my dad was very bitter about all kinds of things. But it wasn't the bitterness that made him a Mexican. It was the bitterness that made him not want to be an American, not want to be an Anglo, and not want to learn English. Mexican me, that was my dad's side

My mother, on the other hand, was born in San Antonio. Her parents, Ignacio Fuentes and María del Refugio Casas, were Mexicans from the Monterrey, Nuevo León, Mexico—the outlying area of Villa de Santiago. I never met my grandfather who died before I was born. My grandmother was Mexican all the way through. My mom went to school in Crystal City, but only to the eighth grade, and then dropped out because of prejudice at school and on the school bus. When mother's family relocated from San Antonio to Crystal City, they lived on the outskirts of town in *el swiche,* or River Spur, on a little *ranchito* that had cows, chickens, goats, hogs, lambs, pigeons, even a mule. It was very hard for her and her siblings to ride the school bus with Anglos. They would be called names and made to sit in the back of the bus. Sometimes the bus would not stop for them if they were still walking toward the pick-up spot. They felt discriminated against, so she quit school.

My mother realized that I needed English to succeed in school. My mother's generation learned very quickly that they had to learn English. The Anglo-controlled public school system had a qualification for the world of learning: you have to know English. If you did not know English, you would fall behind and be pushed out of school. Then you would be called a dropout.

The school across the street from my house was the Mexican school, *la Zavala*. Chicano kids would enter that school and be placed in *zero bola* because they did not know English. *Zero bola* was like minus zero grade! Then they were passed to *primero bajo,* low first, then *primero alto,* high first, *segundo bajo,* low second, *segundo alto,* high second, and finally, the third grade, *tercero,*—if they knew English by then. A kid could be twelve years old and just getting into the third grade. At twelve and thirteen, most boys are growing peach fuzz, if not a moustache. Girls that age begin to become young women; they do not look or act like little girls. The Mexican kids dropped out of school rather than be made fun of by the younger kids who knew English. My mom made it a point that I learn English. She sent me to Suse Salazar's barrio school to learn Spanish and English, to learn to read and do math in both languages. On Friday's, Miss Salazar would make us recite the alphabet, vowels and consonants, multiplication tables, and read poetry or short stories in both languages. We would draw geometric designs and make measurements with rulers she provided. The rulers also were used as a disciplinary device. One by one we would stand facing her at a short distance with our hands out, palms up, and if we made one mistake, her fistful of rulers would come crashing down on our little hands. Ouch! Ouch! And we had to start all over again until we got it right without mistakes. If we got it right, we were treated to the Kool Aid ice cubes she made and, for a penny, had a chance to look at pictures in her View Master.

My mom subscribed to English-language newspapers, *The San Antonio Light* and the local *Sentinel.* She also subscribed to *Look, Life, Reader's Digest, Cosmopolitan,* and the *Ladies Home Journal* magazines. While my dad would make me read his Spanish-language material, my mother would make me read and discuss the English-language material with her. Sometimes when pharmaceutical salesmen would make a business call to my dad's office, he would call me over. My father also knew how to speak English, French, Latin, and some German. He just pretended he didn't understand. He would ask me to translate and interpret what they were saying. It was all a ploy. He was just checking to see if I was on top of all of this. My mother made sure that I knew English. Once I was enrolled in the public school, she was always on top of me about my grades, homework, and studying. Now, that's not the other me. That's how I acquired the English language. The other me is being Anglo. I had to go to school with Anglos, even though the segregated schools were there for Mexicans; my parents refused to allow me to be set apart from the Anglo kids. Somehow my parents enrolled me into the grammar school, the white school. Because of the early childhood education I had received from Suse Salazar, I was moved to the second grade in a matter of weeks. I already knew how to read and write in English.

At the Anglo school, the teachers were also trying to make Anglos out of all of us. That is the whole point of public education in the United States. Students of all kinds have to learn how to be of one kind, Anglo, to stay in and succeed in that system. This was very contradictory for me because the teachers first subtracted from me all my Mexicanness. They took away my language. I was punished if I spoke Spanish in school or on the playground during recess. They took away my culture. I had to eat Anglo food, speak English, learn their stories, songs, and dances. They took away my history. They didn't want to hear about my dad and Pancho Villa—he was a bandit to them. They made me choose between Davy Crockett and Mexican President Antonio López de Santa Anna. They took away everything that was important to me and certainly important to my father. In its place they put in shame and rejection for everything Mexican, me included. And this was very dangerous ground. Here the school was asking me to negate what my father was all about. So, I had to keep this quiet. What I was learning and doing in school was not what I was going to report to my dad at all. And I couldn't discuss this with anybody else either. The students who were being pushed out of school, those who couldn't assimilate and integrate, also looked down on us. They made a choice and were paying the price for keeping their Mexicanness. They called students like me *agabachados, gringo*-like, trying to be white. If you raised your hand to answer a teacher's question, the other Chicano students would glare at you with eyes that spoke, "Why are you playing their game?" Competing with the Anglo students was perceived as selling out the Chicano group, breaking ranks and solidarity. It was an act of Chicano resistance not to play the Anglo's game and speak English or show that you were smart.

We purposely dumbed ourselves down into ignorance. Better to be a dropout than a *vendido lambiscón*, a brown-nosed sellout.

The ultimate rule of the public school game was that Chicano kids had to become Anglo-like to succeed. That was very difficult. A Mexican cannot become white and Anglo-like and remain a Mexican. We were not allowed to be both, nor were we allowed to choose to stay in school. So, we either dropped out or became white, Anglo-like, from the time the 8:00 AM bell rang to the afternoon dismissal. At that time, the Anglos drove off to the their homes, while we walked to our homes in the opposite direction. We also had segregated residential areas. This is the Anglo me.

Once we began walking home from school and before we reached home, we opted for a middle ground. The third me is being Chicano. Being really me. Out in the street, we didn't talk about the three me's. We didn't quite understand that we were being asked to be three people in one: Mexican by our parents, Anglo by the teachers, and Chicanos by ourselves.

We would talk to each other about the teachers and Anglo students who were nasty to us, the discrimination, the problems and troubles we were having at home and in school. Our talk, our language, was neither Spanish nor English; it was a hybrid, both languages made into one: Tex-Mex, Chicano talk. There were no Chicano teachers in school to mentor you. There were some nice white teachers and lots of nasty, mean white teachers, but no Chicano teachers. In high school, I finally met some Chicano faculty: a Spanish teacher and an assistant football coach. Diamantina Rodríguez was the Spanish teacher, and Juan Rivera was the assistant football coach. Later, there were some more, but those are the ones that I remember at the beginning. They didn't give you any kind of advice, though. They certainly did not speak Spanish to us out of the classroom, ever. Consequently, many of us began to think and accept what Anglos, both students and teachers, said about us being too dumb. The teachers were mostly white. All the principals were white. The head coach, superintendent, band director, office people—all were white. The Mexicans were janitors, and some worked in the cafeteria as help. The important people were white. The pretty people who dressed well and smelled good were white. I would look at my female teachers and wish that I could marry one just like them when I was grown up. I knew that when I had children, my babies would look white. I thought in white. I even imagined that God was white, an Anglo. And to make matters worse, the baby Jesus figure I saw at the Sacred Heart Catholic Church did look like an Anglo baby. Even the angels looked like Anglo babies. And I was an altar boy who got to hold them up close and examine those little statues. It didn't take long for me to realize that I was the other. Not Anglo, not Mexican, but what?

When my dad would take me to Mexico to visit relatives, my cousins would make fun of me. They would say that I was a *gringo*, that I was a *pocho*. If you don't know how to speak Spanish properly, like they do, you are called a *pocho*. I didn't know the ways of Mexico. I didn't even dress or look the part with my blue jeans, tennis shoes, and T-shirts. I didn't know what certain foods were. I didn't know any songs in Spanish. I couldn't sing the Mexican national anthem. So they made fun of me. And the whites made fun of us in the same way. We didn't speak English correctly. We didn't even know how to say the Pledge of Allegiance or sing their national anthem either. Same thing. Same thing because both sides were pulling you away from what you were. The Mexicans wanted you to be a Mexican, and the Anglos wanted to make an Anglo out of you. Yet, neither would accept you. So the way we figured it out, at least I did, the Mexicans didn't like us and the whites didn't like us, so we had to like ourselves. And that's where that Chicano me began developing. I liked myself. Being Chicano meant we could have our own music, our own culture, our own way of style, dress, food, music—you name it. And that was the niche that we created because we were different. We were not from Mexico; we were from here in Texas, and that was in the United States now. And we were not made to feel as if we were from here because we weren't accepted, but we still were physically here. We were not going back to Mexico. This was Mexico to my generation. So we were the generation that developed the concept that this was home. That's a very radical concept. When you think you belong, you will fight for what you deserve. And that's exactly what happened with my Chicano generation.

As teachers subtract the Mexican from you, they leave a void that seeks filling with something else. Our parents want that to be filled with Mexicanness. The electronic media, however, continues to maintain this is an Anglo world. The movies, the television shows, the music, the billboards, the advertising, the sports, the newspapers and magazines, and the books are all for Anglos. Even the programs and information in print about us is for them to understand us, not really for us by us. On the Chicano side, since you can't be Mexican and you can't be Anglo, we're always lacking in self-esteem. Nobody validates being Chicano. In fact, that identity is depreciated. Mexicans and Anglos despise the word Chicano; considering it a derogatory term. It's only recently that the English dictionary has put Chicano in the listing. Chicano is defined as a person born in the U.S. of Mexican ancestry.

Within my family, I had to know how to behave in any given situation. Each family always has several generations within it. You've got grandparents, parents, brothers, sisters, cousins, and so you have a range of beliefs. Some family members are more assimilated than others. Some have intermarried with whites or others. I have, in my family, people married to whites, Blacks, Mexicans, and Salvadorans. It's a whole mixture. The younger children, raised in Michigan and Illinois, maybe even in San Antonio. I've met some of my younger cousins and their children. They want to be anything but Mexican. They think Mexican is a derogatory name. They are not proud of it. They want to be Anglos, Hispanics, or Latinos. They want to be something else. And when you have mixed marriages in families, you have people that go out of their way to not offend the non-Mexicans. My older uncles, Tíos Juan and Ignacio, married white women from Tennessee and Kentucky respectively when they returned to the states after World War II. They could not bring their white wives to Crystal City. The local Anglos would not accept that.

My youngest aunt, Tía Lucía, married a Swedish guy. Her children grew up thinking they were white. Not one of them learned to speak Spanish. Some of us even stopped speaking Spanish in front of them, because they did not understand. Parents told us that we would offend them if they did not know what we were saying. Well, what about their whole culture offending us? Why do we have to be the ones to apologize and cut back our identity? Why do people subtract from us and our being, as opposed to them adding our cultural component to themselves? They did marry into our family. They get privileges, and we don't. It's very hard to have mixed marriages within your family because you're always being told not to offend them and, in fact, to make them feel better and join them. That was always very difficult for me.

My uncle, Jesús, presented a different reality. He moved to Monterrey, Mexico and raised his kids as Mexicans. They were born in the United States but hardly spoke English. They are hard-core Mexicans. They still live in Monterrey, but some of them have business in Texas. My other aunts, Antonia and Susan, have children, mostly sons. Their sons have children and they do not speak Spanish.

I grew up in a very unique environment, a very loving environment. My parents both doted on me and everything I needed was always there. They chartered a life path for me. My dad, I'm sure, wanted me to be a doctor. I realized early on I didn't want to be a doctor. But you want to support your parents in their decisions, not disappoint them. I wanted to accept their decisions as my decisions, but it was hard when my dad wanted me to be a Mexican and my mom wanted to make me an Anglo. It's tough.

Now that I have grandkids from my own kids, I want to support them. They know that I'm a Chicano or a Mexican. I think that we're kind of evolving into just being Mexican. Some of them don't want to be Mexican. My daughter Avina was born in Piedras Negras, Coahuila, Mexico. The others were born in the United States and they run the gamut. My oldest son, Adrian, doesn't want to be a Chicano. I don't think he identifies with the term or my position. Although he was raised during the heyday of the Chicano Movement, he was not in it like his parents were. He is more like a true American, all patriotic and right wing in his politics. My daughter, Tozi, since her return to Texas, has become more fluent in Spanish and has adapted culturally. My older children from Luz, my first wife, were mostly raised in Oregon. Oregon is a very white environment. Olin and Avina attended all their public schools in Oregon and Washington. They had little exposure to the Texas Chicano culture. Olin and Avina are both back in Texas now and struggling with Spanish and the *Tejano* culture. I've got two other daughters, Lina and Andrea, who probably would say they are Hispanic or Latina if you asked them. I know they know how to speak Spanish, but they won't. They will only speak Spanish if they know you don't speak English and they have to. Clavel, my youngest, will blurt out her Spanish any way she can without regard to pronunciation, grammar, word choice, accent, or fit. She really wants to be a Mexican. So, they run the gamut.

Now, my grandkids, especially the ones who are the product of my oldest son and his African American wife, Saundra Davison, have troubles with identity. The youngest, Che Nicolás, looks Mexican but wants to be black. He imitates Michael Jackson in singing and dancing and likes his hair in a "Fro." The African-looking one, Adrian Jr., wants to be Mexican, but since childhood we've called him "Bro." When he's asked his name, he correctly pronounces Gutiérrez. Their appearance is confusing for them, as is their identity. People, it seems, are determined to make a person choose one identity. Being mixed is not allowed. These grandchildren ask me sometimes, "What am I, Grandpa? What am I?" Or "How come the kids call me *negro* and they call me names?" It's very, very difficult to deal with kids who are split between two cultures. The answer to my grandkids has been "Blaxican," as a humorous, but accurate way, to respond to that question.

When we were in Oregon somebody slurred Adrian. He came home perturbed and asked me, "Dad, what's a spic?" Before I answered, I had him explain the incident. He said some girls liked him but asked, "Well, are you a spic?" And he told them he didn't know what a spic was. And they said, "Well, you know, a kind of Mexican." He said, "Well, yeah, I am Mexican." So they turned on their heels and walked away from him. Then and there he realized there was some negative connotation to the words "spic" and "Mexican." Andrea and Clavel are always reacting to people telling them, "Well, you don't look Mexican." And they are forever saying, "What's a Mexican supposed to look like? I mean, why can't we come with green eyes and have freckles?" They both have green eyes and freckles. They get those features from their grandparents. Gloria's dad had green eyes and my dad had hazel eyes. My mother and maternal grandmother had green eyes. Mexicans are of various native Indian stocks mixed with all kinds of people who have invaded Mexico over the centuries. We come in all colors of skin, hair texture, eye color, size, shape, weight, and facial appearance. Some of us have lots of body hair; others little or nothing. Some of us had red, brown or blonde hair and are now balding; others still have jet-black straight hair and are seventy years old. Some of us wrinkle, and others do not until they are really old. Some of us have big ears and fat noses, others thin straight noses and little ears. We have round, long, thin, fat, chubby, square, and angular faces. Some of us are tall while others are short. Yet, we are all Mexicans or the children of Mexicans.

We seem to always be taking away from people as opposed to adding to people. When I went to school with Suse Salazar, she was adding on to me. She was adding reading, multiplication, subtraction, measurement, the metric system, geography, literature, history, and English. All that was added to me. When I got to the public school, I was pretty whole and complete—knowledgeable and competent in both languages. Only because of the add-on English and other learned skills from the Spanish into English language was I able to survive. The kids who only came whole in Spanish and without skills had the Spanish subtracted from them. They were going to be pushed out of that school and would probably not succeed. I wish that all adults would learn that adding is much better than subtracting from young people.

I once gave a talk at Bowie High School in El Paso and mentioned that the roots of our Spanish language have so many windows to our cultural heritage and history. The very Spanish that a lot of people want to put down and take away is pregnant with culture. For example, the words that start with "*al*" like *alambre, algodón, alfombra*, and *alcóhol*, all of those are Arabic in origin. Even when we say *ójala*, we are praising Allah. It means "Allah or God is willing." These words date to the Muslim occupation of Spain. The Moors were in Spain for eight hundred years, from 711 to 1492. So was their religion of Islam and their Arabic language. How many of us here in the United States that speak Spanish know that about 17% of the words in Spanish have an Arabic base? Thus, the Spanish that we speak, even though we get chastised for not speaking proper Castillian, is two languages in one. The Spaniards came with their Moorish influences and conquered the Americas beginning in 1492, and they picked up all the indigenous languages. Words like *patata, mesquite, chile*, or *guajolote* are not Irish or European. These words came from the Americas. So did *chocolate, molcajete, metate, tomate, chicle* and *aguacate*. These words are Mayan and Nahuatl. All of the "te" words basically are Meshica words, the Aztec language, also called Nahuatl. When asked, people in those ancient times said they were Meshicanos, which is the origin of Mexicano and Chicano.

And then, of course, you are reading this in English. That's four languages we speak and understand: Arabic, Nahuatl, Castilian Spanish, and English. And in the street, as I mentioned before, we picked up our own jargon, our own hip way of talking, and that's the Spanglish, Tex-Mex, or Chicano language: *chale, simón, nel, taco, chaqueta, traque, troca, carro, faxear, frikear, pistear,* and *shutear,* for example. And clearly adding on, not subtracting, is the future for us who speak five languages. We are pentilingual.

As I write this chapter, I'm on a cruise ship heading back to the United States from Cozumel, Quintana Roo, Mexico. It's amazing that the crew on this ship, about six hundred people, all speak three or four or five languages each. It's just utterly amazing that there are so many people with so many abilities. They are serving you coffee and you can talk to them *en español*. They understand. They are selling you a T-shirt and you can talk to them in English, Thank you, or French, *merci*, or Italian, *grazie*. They understand. It is just so amazing to know that many wonderful people from all over the world. Clearly being multilingual, being a world citizen, being an immigrant, being Mexican, in this case, is a window to the future. The monolinguals, the people who refuse to learn about anybody else and learn only in English, are a dying breed.

These are the three me's: Mexican, Anglo, and Chicano; me, myself, and I.

Learning

I like to learn. Sometimes I do not like the things I learn, but I learn them anyway. It is always better to know why you do not like something. When you like something, you go with it, just feeling good without thinking. Both types of learning are good for you. Learning occurs in many places. School is one place where you can learn. There are other places, such as while talking with people and friends, while traveling, reading, watching people, and, most importantly, listening. I learned a lot listening to my father and mother. They both knew a lot about many things, places, events, people, and history. They each knew different things also. My mother knew English and about *Cristal* and Texas, for example. She also knew about bad Anglos she called *gringos*. My dad also called them that because they did not like Mexican people or their children. My mom knew how to cook really well, how to take x-rays of bones, how to run tests in a medical laboratory, how to help deliver a baby, how to milk cows, and how to care for a garden with grass, fruit trees and lots of flowers. My dad knew about the Mexican Revolution and Mexico. He knew how to drive a big car and shoot guns and the big rifles he owned. He let us do that with him when we went to the rancho. My dad knew how to cure people when they were sick; he was a medical doctor. He was the only Mexican I knew that was a doctor. He knew about medicines, medicinal plants and foods that are good for you. He knew lots of stories and would tell them to me. He knew how to play dominoes, checkers, chess, Sorry, Clue, cards, *lotería,* and bingo. Sometimes at night, especially when it rained or the weather was too cold to sit outside, the three of us would play these games.

When I was about five or six years old, my parents decided it was time for me to go to school. They enrolled me in a private, bilingual school in my hometown sometime in 1950. I think they paid $2.00 a week for my classes. It was before I went to kinder- garten with Anglo kids. The school was run by Suse Salazar and called *La escuelita de Suse Salazar*. Suse's name was Azucena, but we all had to call her "Miss Salazar." After she told everyone to sit down the first day of class, she said that was her name. We were to call her by that name. She was very clear that she did not want any of us to say *"oyes, tú"* or *"oiga,"* much less "hey." Miss Salazar was the proper and only name to call her, plus we had to raise our hand to be recognized. Only then, could we walk up to her and speak privately about our business, such as ask for permission to go to the bathroom or get a drink of water. She told us not to disturb others with private, personal business. The only public questions or com- ments allowed were those about class projects, assignments, math problems, and other school matters. No talking was allowed while in class; that is why we had periods for recess, snacks, and lunch.

That very first day of class she explained *en español* why Chi- cano kids pronounce "Miss" with a long drawn out "I" that sounds like an "E," as in Meeees. She then rattled off a few more words Chicano kids mispronounce, such as cheeeekan (chicken), Share (chair), shurch (church) and, my favorite, shatop (shut up). I thought that was how you did pronounce those words in English. Wrong! She explained that our tongues were trained differently because we spoke Spanish. We were now going to train our tongues to contin- ue to speak Spanish and also learn English. We would move our tongues in two ways and become twice as good.

Miss Salazar taught us a little bit about the English language. She said it was spoken backwards from Spanish. She gave us exam- ples we could readily understand. She then asked if anyone could name the president of the United States of America. Nobody knew. She also asked if anyone knew where he lived. Somebody said in a house or up north or something like that. She laughed. No, that was not it. Miss Salazar was a very large woman. When she laughed, her big belly moved up and down, and her fat cheeks and neck would wiggle and shake like Jell-O. She told us the answer: the president lived in the White House in Washington, D.C. She then made us pronounce all those words—White House, Washington, D.C.—until she thought we had it right. She then asked how anyone would say White House in Spanish. Some of us knew enough English to say *Casa Blanca*. Her eyes got big with eyebrows going up and down with a bunch of, *"Sí, sí, sí, sí . . . ¡Correcto!"* coming out of her mouth. Then, slowly, with a pudgy finger as if she was writing in the air, she said, "House, White. Backwards. See?" *El caballo blanco* became the white horse in English, another example of backward talk that I recall.

I don't remember everything that happened while I was in Suse Salazar's school, but I do remember a lot of things from this first day. On my first day in her school she made a lifetime impression on me. The school was inside a small grocery store. She sold groceries while she taught class. Sometimes a mysterious woman would come in through the back screen door that led to the patio and outhouse. This other woman and her daughter about the age of my youngest aunt, Lucía, would come in quietly and attend to the customers. The front door to the store and our school had a bell that rang when the door was opened. That was the signal for the other woman or her daughter to come see who that was: late student or shopper. The students sat in the middle of the store area, about thirty of us.

Everything in that store was arranged in sections. On one wall she had dried weeds. I thought they were weeds, but they were medicinal herbs. My dad and mom corrected me on that when I told them she had weeds hanging and in jars on shelves. My parents pointed out to me the different teas that we drank for coughs, stomachaches, diarreah, and pain. There were lots of canned and boxed goods on the shelves around us. When class was boring, instead of daydreaming, I would study the pictures and words on the cans and boxes, trying to figure out what was inside of them. She had big barrels with beans, rice, and corn and smaller containers with sugar, salt, white flour, and also tins of lard in all sizes. In another corner, she had sacks of white flour, beans and potatoes.

There was a little room by the front door. I could never figure out what it was for other than secret stuff she sold. The door to the little room was always closed, but it had windows; we could see when she went inside and she could see us, but we never knew what she did while she was in there.

The yard was an outdoor paradise. It had flowers, shade and fruit-bearing trees, a water faucet (sometimes with the hose attached), outhouse, bushes, cactus and a dog. Once outside, a student could explore the wonders of the yard, but not for long, because Miss Salazar would yell out your name from the back door, asking if you were done and telling you to come back inside.

Our desks were apple crates that stood upright, and we sat on little stools. Some students used their shoe-shine boxes to sit on instead of stools. The wooden crates were perfect because they had a piece of wood in the middle that was used as a shelf for our supplies. A carpenter friend of our family, Catarino Castillo, made my little stool. Class would begin early in the morning. My dad would drive me over and admonish me to listen carefully and learn. School would let out in mid-afternoon and my dad would either pick me up in front or I would walk half a block to Canela's Bakery on the corner or look for his car across the street at the Músquiz Café. My dad liked to go have coffee with the owner and his wife, Jesús and Virginia Músquiz. I liked that because they had a daughter my age, Elda, and we would play.

We had to learn the vowels and multiplication tables in Spanish and English. On Fridays, we would get a Popsicle treat if we got a perfect score on our recitation. The Popsicle treat was frozen Kool-Aid in ice trays from her refrigerator. My favorite was grape. If we were exceptionally good, we could see pictures in her View Master, a portable slide-show apparatus, for free or we could pay a penny. She had slides on the Seven Wonders of the World, the airplanes from World War II, Mighty Rivers of the World, the Egyptian Pyramids, and Snow White and the Seven Dwarfs.

We had to recite in both languages, English and Spanish, read stories, and do math in our heads. She would ask us to add, multiply, subtract and divide numbers on paper, and then do it in our heads. It was fun to see how long you could answer questions without making a mistake. The students listening who could point out your mistake were also rewarded with a Popsicle or a turn with the View Master. The older students always caught the mistakes, but Miss Salazar would give everybody a chance to speak up.

My favorite daily routine was to raise my hand and ask permission to go outside to *el cuartito,* the outhouse. I loved to stay out there, looking at the animals and bugs, sometimes I would steal oranges off the tree. Once in a while I would forget to go to the bathroom, and then I was really in trouble when I had to ask to go outside again.

When my parents put me into the Anglo kindergarten, I did not stay there long. The teacher told my parents I knew too much and should be in regular school, but I was too young. A student had to be seven years old before school started to be in the first grade. I remember that I was eventually put into Zavala Elementary, across the street from my house. It must have been around 1951 or so. Zavala was the segregated school for Mexican children. The school people said the Mexican children had to attend a separate school because they did not know English and would hold the other students back if the teacher had to help them learn the language. My mother refused to let me attend more than a couple of days. She insisted they test me in English. They finally tested me and, of course, transferred me to the Anglo school called the Grammar School. After twenty-five days or so in the first grade, I was put in the second grade. I knew too much. I could read, write, spell, do math, recite the Pledge of Allegiance and sing "The Star Spangled Banner." Those things were very important to Anglos. I was promoted again to the third grade ahead of time.

I attended a segregated school for junior high. Anglos and Mexicans were in the same school but in separate classrooms. This was Airport Junior High. Zavala was segregated as a separate building. The Anglo students were in all-Anglo classes. We were in all-Mexican classes. In a conversation with my parents about school at Airport Junior High, they figured out that I was segregated once more. And again, my mother complained. This time it did not work completely. I was moved out of the all-Mexican classes and placed with some Anglo students. The Anglo students were not very smart for lack of attending kindergarden. I was better off in the all-Mexican classes because we were all smart, but I did not say anything to my parents. Fortunately, a brand-new middle school was built during my seventh grade, Sterling Fly Junior High. At Fly Junior High many of the classes had Anglos and Mexicans, but some classes were still all Mexican.

It was during these middle years that I learned that being Mexican was less than being Anglo. I came to that conclusion after being made to speak only English, reading the books about U.S. history, listening to Anglo teachers talk, and watching what was going on in my town on both sides of the railroad tracks that kept us apart. But I fully realized something was wrong when my Anglo friends, girls mainly, told me I could not play with them anymore. When I heard that the first time, I did not understand. When I heard it a second and third time, I understood. I felt hot, like being slapped in the face. I certainly could not touch them anymore. My mother explained to me that the separation was because boys were becoming young men and girls were becoming young women, and it was better to grow apart. It had nothing to do with being Mexican. I didn't believe her. I wished my mother would go to school and see for herself. My father passed away when I was in the seventh grade, so I could not ask him. I was particularly hurt by these words coming from Lynn Pegues. When my dad would take his car to be serviced at the Sinclair gas station, I would always cross the street and play with her in their garage. She was the most beautiful girl in the whole school, and she liked me. I had first met her in the Anglo kindergarten and later would see her at the Grammar School, so it was difficult to understand that we could not play together.

I had my first arguments about Mexico and Mexicans during Texas history lessons. I spoke up against what was stated in the textbooks. I simply narrated what my dad had told me about the so-called Texas Independence Movement and the heroes of the Alamo. I asked the history teacher if these men were not the real "wetbacks." I asked if these Anglos had not stolen the land from the Mexican people. My teacher loudly protested. He said my questions were insulting, so did some of my classmates. They expressed shock and anger that I would say such a thing. In my English classes in junior high and high school, I asked why we never read or studied anything written by Mexicans or in Spanish. I was actually told that those people had never written anything of importance, like the works of Shakespeare and Frost and Browning. How I wished that I could bring my father and Miss Salazar to my classes for a day to set them straight. I learned not to argue, just to raise the questions. My Chicano classmates would ask me after class what I was talking about, and I would tell them what I had learned elsewhere. They believed me.

I had several other firsts during these junior high years: first dance, first fistfight, first girlfriend, and first heartbreak. I always liked girls, but my favorite became Ofelia Perales. She had long, long, brown curly hair, big round brown eyes, and the prettiest walk. Girls used to wear petticoats then, and her skirt would just sway like a giant pendulum clock when she walked. She and her hair always smelled so good. She painted her fingernails, even her toenails, and wore lipstick. To me she was just beautiful. We would meet upstairs in the balcony of the Guild Theatre on Saturday or Sunday. I would walk home after the movies with the taste of lipstick on my mouth, but I was careful to wipe it all off before I got home so my mother would not ask questions. Ofelia was my girlfriend until I met Minerva Tamez; Ofelia was also seeing another classmate when I was not around. Minerva lived by the Grammar School across the street, and her sister, Mary, was my classmate. After school, I would walk over to the Grammar School and pretend to be playing baseball with the guys or doing something so she would notice me. When she would come outside and walk over, I would join her. We would sit on the school playground equipment and talk. She smelled good too, I recall it was the Pond's almond-scented hand lotion. Minerva did not paint her nails or wore lipstick; her mother would not let her. Minerva always smiled, showing off her pretty straight teeth. I liked her a lot.

When I began to drive, on Dollar Night, I would go to the drive-in movies between Crystal and Carrizo Springs. There I met more girls and got into fights with guys from Carrizo Springs and Crystal City over these girls. I began to learn about relationships and how possessive guys and gals are about each other. I felt my first heartbreak with Anna Rojas. She was my best friend, Francisco Rodríguez's cousin. Anna's dad had left them, so her mom moved to San Antonio for better job opportunities. Before they moved, I started going out with Anna when I would visit Francisco.

Anna always insisted I take her for a ride in my car. We would go for ice cream, sodas, or to teach her how to drive. She really wanted to be alone with me. She knew that I liked her tremendously. Anna was a very, very beautiful girl, but she was only ten and I was fourteen. Anna had full lips that made a most kissable mouth, like she was puckering up all the time. She was maturing faster than other ten-year-olds. Her face was perfect, as was the rest of her. But when you are young, four years are a big difference. I thought she was too young for me. After they moved to San Antonio, Anna would visit during holidays and summers. I seldom saw her during the summer months of my high school because I was working as a migrant worker; but I did go out with her during holidays when she would visit. I did not know what love was then, but I sure felt more different with Anna than with any other girl. And when she was gone, I missed her a lot. I was always heartbroken when I thought of her and would see her in my mind.

When I was in college, I found out that Anna had gotten married. When I got married, I found out Anna was divorced. When I was divorced, Anna had remarried. We were like Romeo and Juliet, star-crossed lovers for a long, long time.

I learned firsthand what going steady meant when I had to fight a guy because I had spoken to his girl at the concession stand. He kept telling me that he was going steady with her. And I kept asking, "So?" At the first dances I attended, I learned to spot which girls were with which guys by the way they danced. If you asked someone's girlfriend to dance, a fight was sure to erupt. If you asked a girl outside during the intermission and some guy also wanted to hit on her, you had a fight on your hands. Guys always resort to violence to fix things, making things worse actually, instead of talking it over like the girls do. Fights between boys then were with fists; we didn't even kick each other much, just punches. Some of the bad guys in gangs used knives, chains, bats, pipes, and all kinds of other weapons, but not guns. The grown men used knives and guns. I have always been a large kid and unafraid, so I seldom got the worst in a fight.

My high school years were more of the same, except the Mexican students became the majority of the student body. It was integrated as a building, but segregated in the classrooms. In this school, Anglos took college preparatory classes such as physics, chemistry, plane geometry, trigonometry, and competed in various activities sponsored by the Interscholastic league, such as debate, slide rule, and one-act plays. The Mexican students were mostly in all-Mexican classes, and those were vocational programs, such as shop, welding, mechanics, agriculture and woodworking. Some Anglos, the male children of ranchers, took agriculture class, because they had large animals they raised and sold at the annual livestock fair and show. None of us had that kind of money or rancher dads to keep such animals.

I went to high school from 1958 to May 1962, when I graduated. In between those years, I saw the student body change from Anglo majority to Mexican majority. The rules for electing students to school positions, such as homecoming queen, yearbook staff, school paper editor, most handsome, most beautiful, class president, and student body president also changed. I saw them change. For years, the most repeated democratic message in classes was that the majority ruled, 50 percent plus one vote of those voting. I heard that in every civics class and witnessed the application of the rule in student elections in grammar, junior high, and the first two years in high school. Then it changed. When Chicano students became the numerical majority, the rule changed. The new rule was not fair. I got the message: Mexicans were to remain the minority regardless. The school authorities left majority rule alone, but changed the qualifications for holding such school positions as class president and the other favorite selections. They posted grade levels and grades as qualifications. They required parents of candidates to have been graduates. Teachers and other out-of-town persons became the judges for selection of our favorites. Teachers and other school authorities would count the "secret" ballots. None of the students were allowed to watch the count or question it. They moved the election dates to when many migrants were still out of school. I did not know of a single Anglo that was a migrant. I learned that you could determine the outcome of any election if you rigged the qualifications to favor a certain group, as in this case. Just a few of our parents were high school graduates. Most all Mexicans were migrants and left the school program early and/or returned late. Many of us did not have good grades. The number of Mexican students in higher grade levels was much less than that of Anglo students. We dropped out of school. I prefer to say, we were pushed out. Mexican students were becoming the overwhelming majority, and we were beginning to be vocal about injustice. I certainly was.

As candidate for class president my junior year, I returned from migrant work in California in time to ask all Chicano and some Anglo students to vote for me. I also got some Chicano students to encourage several Anglo students to seek the position. What I was doing was simple: dividing the Anglo vote among several candidates and lining up solid support for me. I also went around to the various Anglo candidates and asked if they would vote for me the second time around if nobody got a majority vote the first time. I had learned the tricks of student politics in the years past. I was elected class president both junior and senior years, plus I was elected student body president also.

My favorite experience of that time was winning the state championship in public speaking during my junior year in 1961. I was the first Chicano to win that state title. I spoke about the democratic messages found on the faces of a penny. I still have a copy of that speech in my scrapbook. I was a good speaker thanks to Suse Salazar. I had poise, articulation, enunciation, and a good delivery with enough gestures and voice inflection to win over the judges. They were always Anglos. One or more of the judges in competitions always told me I spoke English so well, that my English was without accent, that I didn't look "Spanish," and that I sounded a lot like a college student. I figured out that all of these statements really meant they were surprised that a Mexican was better than Anglo competitors.

I joined the interscholastic competitions because of the white girls. I saw them practicing poetry reading in the auditorium one day and lingered, listening through an open window. There was no air conditioning at the time. The speech coach, Aston Pegues, insisted I either leave or come in and recite. I was bothering them, he accused me. The girls on stage were some of the prettiest ones in high school, and one of them was Lynn Pegues, my all-time favorite. I went in. He handed me a poem to study and read. It was something entitled, "The Tale of the Spun Glass Ship." I read it when called up, out loud as best as I could. I had not read a poem out loud since my days with Suse Salazar. Mr. Pegues was impressed. He said I was very, very good. And he was the first to say what I was to hear over and over again about my public speaking ability. I signed up for the public speaking competitions and drama, anything that would keep me close to Lynn and the other girls.

After my high school graduation, I went to Southwest Texas Junior College in Uvalde, Texas. I had a lot of trouble there with politics, not classes, because there were a lot of white students who were rednecks. They did not like Mexicans attending classes with them, sitting next to them, eating next to them, and, in our case, coming from Crystal City, riding the bus to and from Uvalde with them. We were made to sit in the back of the bus. More importantly, in Crystal City the Mexican community was organizing to contest the upcoming city and school board elections in the spring of 1963. My high school buddies and I became very involved in that, but it was a very difficult time for me. I met Juan Patlán and Gabriel Gutiérrez from Dimmitt County, and Gabriel Tafoya and Ismael Talavera from Uvalde while attending the community college. We became friends, and they also got involved with Crystal City politics. On campus, I ran for class president and lost in a very ugly campaign. The white students went around tearing down my campaign flyers and posters. They would write nasty comments on my advertisements. I was not allowed to speak to students in the public area. Once I was even threatened with a belt-buckle beating and chased from the dormitory where I was passing out literature. The rednecks wore big belt buckles to hold up their jeans over heavy cowboy-style boots. They took off their belts and used them in a fight. They would kick you with their pointed, hard boots. Fortunately, I had other Chicano students with me and the brawl did not take place.

Dean Jerald Underwood worked actively against me during the campaign, and I went to his office to protest his activities. He not only admitted his involvement but also accused me of being a communist and an atheist. I didn't really know what those words meant in my case. I could not connect the accusations to my beliefs. Underwood told me he had heard from reputable sources in Crystal City what kind of an ungrateful student I had become after all that the Anglos had done for me in my hometown. I was incensed. Not only was he saying I had little to do with my success, but also that I should be thankful to Anglos for the privilege of succeeding. I was astounded to learn that here we were meeting other Chicano students from area communities for the very first time, yet the Anglo students knew each other and the Anglo administrators knew all the influential Anglos in the region for years. They were connected and we were not.

Chicanos won the Crystal City elections, and I got a summer job. This was the first time in years that I was not going north in search of work. I ran a swimming pool in the afternoon and evening and gave swimming lessons in the morning. The new city council ordered the city pool and parks integrated so everyone could swim, cook out, picnic, play ball, and the like in municipal facilities. The Anglos didn't like what was happening. They refused to integrate the city-owned country club and golf course. It was theirs, they argued in court, because they had signed a lease for ninety-nine years with the city before the Mexicans had taken over. The courts upheld them in that contract. We could not attend events in our own tax-supported golf course or clubhouse, except as laborers.

Extreme pressure from the English-language media and internal strife among the Mexican American members of the city council caused things to begin breaking apart. The council members were fighting one another. The mayor and city manager were fighting one another. The newspapers were always saying horribly negative things about our electoral effort and our council members. I was having lots of problems with security and personal safety at the city pool, especially at closing time when I had to run off the drunken Anglos milling around to harass me as I locked the gates and turned off the lights. The new Chicano cops for the city got tired of my calling them to escort me to my car. I started carrying a baseball bat, then a gun, because I carried money, the gate receipts from the day and concession sales.

Finally, I ran away to Los Angeles, California, at the end of the summer. I did not want to return to Uvalde's junior college nor did I want to experience defeat in the next elections. In Los Angeles, I found jobs and made money. I also made political contacts with folks I had met when I was sent out there right after the April city election. I had long conversations with Eduardo Quevedo, one of the founders of the Mexican American Political Association (MAPA). He reminded me of my dad. He was a large man with big hands and ears. He had gray hair and sagging cheeks. He smoked and his suits reeked of smoke, just like my dad. He taught me the history behind MAPA and the group that had helped us in Crystal City, the Political Association of Spanish Speaking Organizations (PASO). Both MAPA and PASO had been formed after the presidential campaign that

Mexican Americans organized in support of John Fitzgerald Kennedy in 1960. Quevedo lamented that the two groups were identical in program objectives but could not negotiate their difference in name and become one. He was the first person to tell me that there were Mexicans who did not want to be Mexicans. I could not fully understand what lesson he was impressing on me. I did tell him that I could recall situations during which Mexicans sided with Anglos against other Mexicans. He said that was almost it, but that those things I mentioned happened mostly over economics: money, jobs, opportunity, and business arrangements.

I enrolled in Los Angeles City College, but I never attended. Instead, I quit my job and came back to Texas to help Virginia Músquiz campaign for state representative. She was the first Chicana to run for such an office in Texas, maybe the entire United States. After that campaign, which she lost, I enrolled at Texas A&I University in Kingsville.

My very first class in government at A&I was municipal government with Professor Ben Hobbs. I made a D in the class. That grade devastated me, and I went to see him about it. He never told me exactly what I had done wrong in my written exam. He advised me that if government was my major, to try harder. He offered me a job as a work-study student—my first real break with financial help to go to school and learn. Professor Hobbs obtained the application for me, helped me fill it out, and hired me. He is now a realtor in Dallas, Texas.

I remember liking government since high school. That's what it was called then. Now the field of study, the discipline, is called political science, but there's no science to it. When humans are involved, there can't be any science. We are not predictable. The scientific method requires predictability and replication. I remember that I was drawn to government courses. Perhaps it was because of the Crystal City experience, the five Mexican-American candidates running for the city council, that I got hooked on politics. Perhaps it was the regular discussions I overheard my dad have with people in the Jesús Gámez and Celestino Menchaca barbershops about Mexican politics, the Korean War, and what was wrong with U.S. foreign policy. My dad did not go to get a haircut that often, but he did go regularly to converse and visit. I would tag along and listen like a fly on the wall. Maybe it was a combination of those things that nurtured my interest in politics. I loved it. I just couldn't get enough of it. While in high school I practiced student politics and organizational politics by running for student government and club offices. I knew government was going to be my major in college, once I figured out what people meant by the words "major" and "minor." I also practiced politics in Kingsville with demonstrations, protests, student government, and clubs.

It did not take me long to hook up with former classmates from the junior college and make new friends with students from other cities in the state, mostly South Texas. The students from Laredo were a unique lot. Invariably, those border students loudly protested our use of the word Chicano as a self-identifier. They were Latin Americans or of Spanish descent. They made fun of our Chicano Spanish and insisted that there were no problems between "Latins" and Anglos. They asserted there was no discrimination. Moreover, they insisted that they had never been discriminated against, ever. I could not believe how naïve they were or blind or just plain in denial with their heads in the sand. I wished that I could board them on an airplane and take them to Crystal City, to the junior college, to West Texas where Mexicans at that time were still run out of restaurants, barbershops, beauty shops, movie theatres, and social clubs. I told them about my experiences, and they scoffed at me. The other Chicanos did not like Laredo students. I guess that is why students from Laredo formed their own Laredo Club on campuses across the state. Maybe they were correct in stating they had never been discriminated against; they stood apart from everyone else.

I began organizing the Chicano students and formed alliances with some Anglo and black students. There were not many black students in South Texas, and the athletic programs then did not recruit black students from elsewhere, like colleges and universities do now. College athletics were for Anglo students in the mid to late 1960s.

At Texas A&I University, Chicano students were in a numerical minority. I had to adjust my tactics and strategies to fit that reality. We could not win anything without the help of others. How do you convince others to support your group and not their groups? You do it one-on-one. I went out and found others interested in what I wanted done. I broadened my agenda to include some of what they were interested in. We protested global concerns, such as the war in Vietnam being fought at that time. We protested against the president of the university and his policies. We argued he worked for us with our tuition and fee money and the tax money our parents paid—we did not attend A&I because of him. This was our school, not his. At A&I in 1965 and 1966, President James Jernigan maintained segregated dormitories. Chicano and black students were forced to take orientation for noncredit but pay for it as a regular course. An English proficiency exam was instituted as a prerequisite for graduation. Off-campus students did not have student body representation. Only English-language music and Anglo food was available in the student center. Students could not sell used books to each other, only to the campus bookstore. Campus dances had English-language music only. I organized a PASO chapter on campus and wanted it recognized as a student organization. It was not. The list of grievances grew to include the concerns of lots of student groups. When I had significant numbers of others and all the Chicano students organized, I called for campus demonstrations against the war, against the student fees and tuition, against the president, against the bookstore, and against discrimination in housing, testing, and curriculum.

I graduated in May of 1966 before subsequent reforms of all our protests were instituted. A&I has changed for the better since then. I went on to law school, but did not find that environment conducive to learning what I wanted to learn. It reminded me of the junior college, with lots of bigoted closed-minded people, including professors. I quit after nine months of law study and began to pursue a graduate program leading to a doctoral degree. Much later, I returned to law school. I still wanted to learn about the law and I did.

I love learning. And in every stage of my life I have learned from others, with others, and from myself engaged with others. I recommend it to you.

Cooking

I love cooking and camping. I like camping because it's a lot of fun being outdoors. I like cooking because I eat. And because I eat, I'm involved with food, agriculture, livestock, and, of course, cooking. I learned how to be a field cook, meaning someone that can take an animal still on the hoof, kill it, dress it, and then cook it. I learned that from my grandma Cuca, María del Refugio Casas Fuentes. I was the only grandchild in Crystal City when she lived alone, so I had to go across town from one end to the other to help her with chores. She lived in México Chico, one of the Mexican barrios in *Cristal*. I lived in México Grande, the other barrio, and main Mexican business section. The other two barrios were Avíspero and Camposanto, where the Mexican cemetery was located. As a child when my parents were living, we would go spend Sunday's visiting grandma. As a teenager around 1957 to about 1961, I would chop her wood, start her fires to heat water, and wash or cook. I would catch and kill the chickens she pointed out to me. Killing goats, pigs, rabbits, sheep and calves was routine for me. I would also tend to her garden and clean out the barn, chicken coop, pig stalls and *corrales*. I did all of those things. My grandmother was a good cook. She made *mole* regularly from roosters she did not want anymore. She made *carne seca*, beef jerky, on the clothesline and *carne asada,* roasts, on the open fire. She made good flour tortillas. Grandma loved sweets. At four in the afternoon, she would announce that it was time for *el hache y hache*. This meant it was time for coffee, the brand was H & H. If she did not have her coffee with *pan dulce* or something sweet, she would get a headache and be in a terrible mood. I never wanted to see my grandmother in a bad mood or even be near her when she was upset. She had a wicked *revés,* a backhanded slap that stung worse than a belt smack.

My grandmother had all the facilities and amenities of a modern kitchen. She had a gas stove, washing machine, water heater, refrigerator with freezer, but she preferred to cook and wash outdoors. If she cooked indoors, it was on a wood stove or the fireplace, not on the gas stove. And she didn't want to use a washing machine. She washed by hand with a washboard in a #8 tub. She made her own soap and cooked her own starch. The only thing she used the washing machine for was to wring the clothes since she had developed arthritis and her hands hurt. She didn't ask me to wring the clothes because she said my hands were always dirty. We would hang up the clothes on the clothesline for the sun to dry them. There's nothing like the fresh smell of clothes dried outdoors. They smell better than those dried with Downy strips in an automatic machine.

My mother was also a good cook. My mother would cook fantastic meals for my father on weekends. During the week my dad did not have dinner. My dad's idea of dinner was hot, sweet bread from Canela's Bakery with a glass of milk. That was all. When I would get home Mom and I would eat a snack. It was always something special, such as Oreo or Hydrox cookies, sweet tortillas, chocolate cake, peach cobbler, ice cream, and occasionally a sandwich. To this day, Oreos, Fig Newtons and chocolate cake are my favorite desserts with a big glass of milk. I don't think they make Hydrox cookies anymore, but they were just like Oreos. Afterward, she and I would eat a regular dinner while my dad savored his *pan dulce con leche.* My mother's *arroz con pollo, enchiladas, carne guisada, caldos,* and *lengua entomatada* are dishes that still make my mouth water just thinking of them as I write this.

On weekends it was a different story. We would have a sit-down lunch and a sit-down dinner. My mother would make elaborate dishes that my dad liked. I remember she would make *riñones, pollo en mole, cesos lampriados, cabrito, puerco con calabaza* and the tastiest pork chops and ribs. She would make steak *ranchero sin chile.* My dad did not like *chile* on his food; my mom and I did. She would make *bacalao a la Vizcaína,* a salty dried fish with olives in a tomato sauce combination. That was my dad's favorite. It was a little too fishy for me, but I have learned since to develop a taste for that. And we ate a lot of fruit. Bananas are still my favorite. We would eat grapes, melons, lots of oranges from our trees in the backyard, peaches, plums, and figs. Watermelon with salt was a summer favorite.

My dad did not like to attend church services. When he did, he sat in the last row in the back and he smoked! No one ever said a word to him. I was embarrassed when he did that, but that was my dad. The local priests, those that spoke Spanish, would come to our house for dinner. My father never invited the English-speaking priests to the house. During Lent, my dad invited the Spanish-speaking *misioneros* over to eat or drink coffee. These *misioneros* usually were priests sent from another area to preach sermons to the congregation over several days. First, the men would be invited to evening service, then the women. I never knew why they could not preach the same thing to everybody. Altar boys were not allowed in those services, so I never really knew what was said.

My mother did attend church regularly and sang in the choir. I took an interest in becoming an altar boy. When I was an altar boy, the priests used to take us to Garner State Park, north of Uvalde, Texas, as a reward and treat. Garner Park was, and still is, a favorite spot of mine. The priests idea of showing us a good time was buying a couple of pounds of bologna, fresh tomatoes, *serrano* peppers, white bread and hot Cokes, and just leaving us out there all day long. We couldn't cook because the grills were only at campsites and cabins, not by the river bottom. Besides, you fix bologna sandwiches, you don't cook them.

I got involved with the Boy Scouts by accident. The kids from my street would play *patada al bote* (kick the can) in the street by Zavala School, which was across the street from my house and covered an entire city block. The game consisted of placing a metal can, usually a coffee can or any big can on the ground under the streetlight. Somebody would be designated "it" and made to count to 50 while the rest of us hid in the dark areas. The "it" person would then go in search of us to tag us. We, in turn, would hide and attempt to return to kick the can, without being tagged by the "it" boy. The one tagged was then "it" and the game would start over. We played this game almost every night and got home sweaty and dead tired from so much running. My favorite buddies were Pete Galván Jr., Gilberto Martínez, and Rudy Palomo. Pete lived across the street from me, and Gilberto lived half a block down on West Edwards. Rudy lived all the way down the same street, almost at the end. Sometimes we were joined by Rudy's cousin, José Alfaro, and Homero Flores, sometimes the Martínez brothers, Lalo and René. They all lived down the street on West Edwards. A block over on Avenue A lived the De la Rosa brothers, Alberto and Homero. Their cousin, Chale de la Rosa, lived a block down on West Edwards. There were a few others who would join us in playing *patada al bote* from down the street or a few blocks away: Efraín, Pete Flores, Chaparro Valdez, sometimes the Vargas kids and the Mojica and Pardo boys. We never invited any girls to play.

There were some big buildings and lots of small plywood barracks used for classrooms with screens and no windows on the school campus. In the winter, the screens of these barracks would be covered with hinged plywood panels. In the summer, these panels would be held open with a stick. There was no heat in these barracks, and they sat high on posts off the ground. There were a few big cranberry trees on the school ground and some laurel bushes between the trees. The barracks and trees and bushes made excellent places to hide while playing *patada al bote*. Sometimes we would just hide under the barracks and wait for lovers to come meet each other there. We would play pranks on them and scare the girls out of their wits.

One evening, those of us playing in the street and schoolyard noticed some sort of meeting going on in one of the barracks. It was a grown man with a bunch of Chicano kids, and they were reciting stuff in English and making knots. They finally came outside to play a game much like our Kick the Can, but they called it Steal the Flag. Each team would post a flag on its side. The teams would then try to sneak past the other team members and find, then steal the flag. If you were captured, you went to the "stockade," a fancy word for jail. We found out they were Boy Scouts, and the man was the mailman, Gerald Saldaña.

When Gerald Saldaña began having meetings in our neighborhood, he attracted attention. Most of the Chicano kids who attempted to join, promptly quit, because they found out they had to buy a uniform and equipment, including a Boy Scout handbook. Mr. Saldaña allowed you to stay in without money, but you had to at least have one item of clothing and the handbook. Most Chicano kids bought the official handkerchief with a knot clasp and wore that as *the* uniform with blue jeans, tennis shoes and T-shirts. Others went to the secondhand surplus store and bought old U.S. Army issue khaki shirts, web belts, canteens, and backpacks. I did that.

I talked to my parents about joining and was given permission. My dad asked me if I knew this was like joining the Mexican Boy Scout troop. I didn't fully understand the significance of that question, and he did not belabor the point. When I told him how poor our troop was in equipment, handbooks, uniforms and supplies, my dad offered to drive to Uvalde and bring back some Boy Scout items. There was a department store in Uvalde that carried such things. He bought several handbooks, patches, some shirts, handkerchiefs, knot clasps and belts with the Boy Scout insignia on the buckle. He gave them to Gerald Saldaña, the scoutmaster, and kept some items for me. My mother sewed the patches on to my Army shirt. I belonged to Troop 93, the Mexican troop from Crystal City. With allowance money, I bought Brasso and polished my buckle. It was really shiny. I memorized the handbook in about a week. I became proficient and fast at knot tying. All the Chicano kids did. It seemed that we were eager to compete with the Anglo Boy Scouts and show them that Mexicans were better. I told the scoutmaster that I was going to be the first Chicano Eagle Scout in Crystal City, but he informed me that three others had already done that in the Anglo troop: Lionel and Jaime Galván and Arnoldo Menchaca. The fathers of these boys worked at the local ice plant.

Most Mexican people did not have electric refrigerators during this time; rather they had iceboxes, which needed a block of ice daily. Ice and milk were still delivered to the doorsteps of homes in the 1950s. Because most families lacked refrigeration, many of them made *carne seca* by placing thin-sliced meat on a clothesline to dry. My grandma and mother made it. They would squeeze lemon juice on and rub salt and pepper into the meat, then put it out to dry in a wire mesh contraption. It looked like a screen torn from a window screen because that is exactly what it was.

Although there were segregated Boy Scout troops in Crystal City and the entire Winter Garden area of South Texas, we did come together to compete. Each troop still had to go on field trips, have meetings, and go camping in order to learn and apply the Boy Scout manual. That's where I learned about camping. I was already learning to cook from my mother and grandmother. I could start a fire with one match or none and boil water in record time. At the multitroop gatherings, there were contests to see which troop members could build the quickest fire, boil water the fastest, tie knots, race and, of course, cook over an open fire. We'd have to make biscuits, pancakes, *pan de campo* (coal-fired baked bread) and baked potatoes. I also became a whiz at making baked potatoes.

Down the street from me, Simón and Ninfa Martínez parents, allowed us to dig a big hole in their backyard. We dug a hole for days until it was large and deep enough for several of us to hide there. We carved a niche on one cave wall for a fireplace and other niches for us to sit in. We made fires in that fireplace and cooked potatoes. That is where I learned how to wrap them in foil and cook them over coals.

Scoutmaster Saldaña took us camping regularly. And we, on our own, would go camping at the Galván Ranch, which was located about five miles north of Crystal City. Pete Galván's family owned a large tract of land by the Nueces River. We'd go there to camp, hunt with our .22 caliber rifles, and swim.

My family owned seventy acres just outside of Crystal City also, but it had no trees or river like Pete's ranch. More importantly, my grandmother lived out there. She was not about to have us building campfires, singing and screaming into the night. The pond was dry and the land was leased for cattle grazing. When grandma traveled to San Antonio for the weekend or to Mexico, we'd invite girls.

Another favorite camping site was the flood plain south of the city. It was called Turkey Creek, and when it rained a lot, a small lake formed just behind the swimming pool area. The place had lots of trees and brush, no houses. It was a great place to pretend to be hunting in a jungle. Those of us from West Edwards would walk over there after a big rain to swim or catch crawfish and shoot rabbits. On the way we would pick up other boys, such as Patricio and Johnny Delgado. Once, we decided to go swimming out there after a big rain. But when we arrived, the Cook sisters were already in the lake. There were two white families that lived in the Mexican side of town, the Cooks and Solanskys. And they were all really blonde with almost white hair, not yellow. The girls had lots of freckles around their big blue eyes and nose, just like their brother, Douglas, who was our age. The other Anglo kids would not mix with them; they called them white trash. I guessed then that white trash meant poor whites, because these two families were very poor. I could tell by their clothes, shoes, and hair. They always looked dirty and unkempt.

While swimming in the small lake on that occasion, I got bit by a crawfish on my right leg just below my knee. The crawfish had my flesh firmly in its claw and would not let go. I pulled on it but it hurt too much. I finally asked for help. One of the older Cook girls came over to me. I told her what the problem was. She tried to pull it off but couldn't, because I would scream in pain. She was tearing the skin off my leg when she pulled the crawfish. It just wouldn't let go. Someone got the bright idea to light a match and hold it near the crawfish to make it let go, but we were in the water. I had to get out of the water naked. We were all swimming naked. The pain was great and I didn't care, neither did the older Cook girl.

The match trick did not work and she finally just pulled it off by wiggling it side to side. The crawfish kept part of my leg in its claw. The girl placed a mud pack on my leg and held it there until the bleeding stopped. I still have the scar on my right leg. And the memory of that naked, full-grown girl right in front of me as well. Gilberto, Pete and the others thought I was a funny sight, but they also still have the memory of that girl. We have talked about that experience from time to time as adults.

Because of all these early experiences, a few of us in the Chicano Boy Scout Troop were great competitors at Boy Scout Jamborees. We would usually outperform the Anglo Boy Scout troops. I remember attending a Baptist Rio Frio camp and paying for my stay by serving as a dishwasher and assistant cook. I had also worked at the Del Monte Camp, a Bracero Program, as a dishwasher. I watched how they cooked large amounts of food for people, such as chicken in salsa and hamburger meat, *picadillo,* and *carne guisada.* My cooking was limited to help run the corn tortilla-making machine.

As teenagers, Ambrosio Meléndrez and I began a competition to see which of us would become the first Eagle Scout from Troop 93. We raced neck-to-neck, earning intermittent ranks and the required number of merit badges to reach our goal. Both he and I were awarded the Eagle Scout rank on May 19, 1959. He was sixteen, and I was fourteen years old. My dad did not live to see that; he had passed away in 1957. My mother attended the ceremony held at the Community Center, a white-only facility in the Anglo part of town, except on this occasion.

During my high school years, we would always go out to the Galván Ranch to drink Jax beer and have cookouts. We were underage, but we had adult connections for the beer and money to buy it, along with food. But it wasn't the hot dog and Spam kind of cookout. No, we actually made bacon and *chorizo.* We actually cooked. We would kill rabbits, wild turkeys, quail, and armadillos and eat them. Later in life when we could afford to buy weapons, we were allowed to hunt with bigger rifles, 30-30's and shotguns,

12 and 20 gauges. Then we killed deer at the people's lease, Highway 83, and hunted wild hogs and javelin.

The years that I attended the Southwest Texas Junior College in Uvalde, I lived alone in the family home in Crystal City. My mother stayed in Chicago with a sister, my aunt Consuelo, to earn more money. I had to cook for myself. My past experience helped a great deal, as it did when I hit senior college at Texas A&I in Kingsville. I usually cooked for any and all of my roommates. My format remains the same to this day. I will cook enough for the entire family, eat some, freeze the rest for meals the balance of the week.

When I was in the Army at Ft. Leonard Wood during my twenties, there were a couple of Mexican cooks in the mess hall. Occasionally, I would get a care package from home, sent either by my mother or my wife, with some *chile,* tortillas, *carne seca,* and spices. I would cook in the mess hall and share. They would let me get in there early Sunday mornings when many soldiers did not wake up or go in for breakfast. We would make *huevos rancheros* and refried beans. Several times, we tried to make flour tortillas but failed miserably. I have never been able to make good *masa* or roll it out in perfect circles like my mother or my first wife, Luz, did.

Once I got into politics as an organizer, leader, campaigner, candidate, and officeholder in Crystal City, my cooking skills greatly enhanced my reputation and standing, especially in the eyes of women volunteers. Women do all the work in political campaigns and get no credit. Women do all the work at home and also get no credit.

At first, the women did not believe I could cook. I did not argue or attempt to convince them. I knew how to kill a pig, for example, and how to clean it. That is a massive job. This is how: You kill the animal by shooting it in the head or with a mighty, sledgehammer blow between the eyes. Hoist it in the air on a beam or tree to dress it, meaning cut it open and take out the guts. Pigs, cows, wild hogs, *javalina,* deer and some big goats are very heavy to pick up. Get help. Then, you boil water and use plenty of burlap sacks or linen cloth. The animal is wrapped or draped with these fabrics, and boiling water is poured over them. As you let it soak a while and you keep pouring boiling water on the cloth, you then remove a section of cloth to scrape the grime, hair and outer skin clean. I use a brick or a piece of 2x4 board held between my hands to scrape the skin with the edge. More hot water, more scraping, more hot water, more scraping until the skin is very clean, almost pinkish, not white-like, because fat is white. Skin is pink and below that is the white fat. The skin is used to make *chicharrones*. The fat with meat is used to make *carnitas*. The pure fat is used to make lard. The pig's head is used to make the meat and lard for tamales, a Christmas favorite among many families. The pig's feet and tail are used to add gelatin and flavor to *menudo*, the breakfast of champions.

Dressing baby goats, *cabritos*, is different. You kill them by cutting their throat and catching the blood in a saucepan, adding salt to keep it from coagulating. Refrigerate the blood until ready to use and make sure no one else adds salt to anything. The goat is skinned and dressed. The guts are used to make other delicacies, such as *machitos* and *tripitas*. The meat is cut into small pieces and cooked in a big pot with onion, a couple of bay leaves, garlic, *comino*, and pepper. When the meat is tender and parting from the bone, you add the blood and mix quickly. The blood cooks instantly in the boiling brew and turns the entire batch black. It looks unusual but tastes delicious.

During the political era in Crystal City in the early 1970s, we used to go to Garner Park near Uvalde and rent cabins. The state park is named after a former vicepresident of the United States, John Nance Garner. We would have cookouts, inside and outdoors. When I attended the Junior College in Uvalde, Mexicans weren't allowed to rent the cabins at Garner State Park. We could enjoy the entire park: trails, caves, camping areas, grassy meadows, river, concessions, boat and horse rides, and the screened shelters, but not the cabins. We saw many Anglo families coming in and out of those stone houses, but not one Mexican. But after the *Cristal* revolt in 1970, we started raising hell about that discrimination, particularly while I was a school board member, and then a county judge.

The state park cabin area was open to all; now it's hard to get a cabin. Cabin reservations are made at the beginning of the year, but issued by lottery. I still love to go there. I wrote my book, *A Gringo Manual on How to Handle Mexicans* there. Maybe I should go back there and write another book. It's a wonderful place, beautiful hilly country with mountain laurel and cedar growing everywhere. The scent of those two trees is pervasive. The water in the Frio River that runs through the park is so clear you can see the fish and the rock bottom. In the early dawn hours in Garner State Park, deer can be sighted grazing in the grassy meadows or lurking at the edge of the hillside.

The downside is that open fires are prohibited. Campers must cook indoors in cabins or outside on the open grills. A portable grill is permitted. I just can't cook on an open grill; the smoke and heat just go up and away, not into the meat. Brisket, ribs, steaks, and chicken don't taste the same if cooked on an open grill. A *cabrito* or any animal can't be killed for cooking and eating in the park.

In Crystal City, I was in charge of directing the cooking operation. There were other excellent outdoor cooks, such as the Salinas brothers, Adolfo "Fito" and Juan. They were football coaches and also very good at cooking fajitas, brisket, *tripitas*, anything on a grill or outdoor fire. They would always be assigned to direct, coordinate, and help because we did a lot of fund-raising by selling barbeque chicken and fajita plates. During Christmas, we would have big *tamaladas* and *barbacoa en pozo* for sale. *Barbacoa en pozo* consists of beef heads washed, wrapped in wet linen cloth or foil, and slow cooked in a hole in the ground. The hole is about four-feet-deep and three feet in diameter and dug days before. Usually the *barbacoa en pozo* is made overnight for an early breakfast. It is important to place two wires around each head to pull them up from the hole when cooked. A hot bundle without wire is very difficult to remove from a hot hole. The heads are placed in a hole in the ground that has been fired up. A fire is started in the hole and kept raging for half an hour or more until the hole and the surrounding dirt is hot. Dropping a few big rocks in the remaining coals in the hole helps, but is not necessary. The heads are placed in the hole. The hole is covered with an aluminum sheet or discarded metal roofing. Dirt is spread over the metal cover to seal the hole completely. Another fire is started over the dirt and metal cover above the hole. The fire is kept raging for an hour or so. Then you forget about it or go make tamales or finish your party. Early the next morning, the ash and dirt are removed from the metal cover and the hole is opened. That first smell is unique. A hook or a hoe is used to pull out the beef head bundles. When the bundles are unwrapped, the meat just falls from the bones.

My favorite meats from the beef head are the tongue and cheek. You have to peel the tough layer of skin from the tongue before you eat it. The meat from the cheek is so delicious and just melts in your mouth. Some people, like my father, eat the eyes, not the pupils, but the meat around them. I like brains. Getting the brains out is very difficult; there's a trick to it. After the meat is removed from the jawbone, one of the bones is used to pry open the back of the head. Where the head is joined to the neck is an opening. The jawbone end that hooks to the head, not the front end where the teeth are, is inserted in that hole and pressed down like a lever. The back plate of the head will come off, exposing the entire brain. Enjoy.

Orders for our prepared plates of food would be pre-sold to ensure financial success and also to determine the extent of support for the candidates and interest in the election. Tamales were sold by the dozen, *barbacoa, tripas,* and *mollejas* were sold by the pound, and chicken, fajitas, and *carne guisada* by the plate with trimmings, rice, beans and sometimes potato salad.

After every home football game and after political events, invariably on a Friday or Saturday, we would have cookouts in people's backyards, or we would go up to Garner State Park and have cookouts there while we were debriefing or planning our political activities. More often than not the cookouts were just for fun. But all that cooking came in handy for me in politics and at home.

Every Friday afternoon I still have a habit of barbequing or grilling for my family. My daughter Tozi and a friend of hers, Dylan, gave me a huge grill, half of a chopped-up, round butane tank with a lid on wheels. It's great for grilling. I could probably cook a quarter cow in there. I used to have a grill that would sit on the ground. I would use a *disco* with it to make *tripitas* and *mollejas*. A *disco* is a round concave piece of metal that comes from a plow. Little legs are soldered on to the *disco* and some cooks add handles for easy transport. *Tripas* are the beef intestines and the *mollejas* are glands. They are washed thoroughly, especially the intestines, and boiled with salt and pepper until cooked and soft. They can then be fried or grilled. The frying or grilling is to make them crunchy and flavorful from the burning wood. Mesquite wood is my favorite for grilling and smoking meat.

All my outdoor cooking equipment is now gone, except the large grill. In all the moving from Texas to Oregon back to Texas, and within Texas, here and there, I have just lost track of all of that, or someone borrowed items and never returned them.

When I took part of my family to Europe in 1978 and again in 1992, I rented a recreational vehicle with a stove, a toilet, beds, and storage space. I also took a Smoky Joe grill. We would go to the local market and buy fresh meat and foodstuffs. Every night, under the stars and the heavens, I cooked all kinds of food for my family. I didn't want to cook inside the motor home. Besides, it smelled everything up. We would cook spaghetti, bacon and eggs, pancakes, rice and chicken, but the grilling, especially the fish, beef, and lamb, I would cook outside.

In Oregon during the early 1980s, when Luz or I couldn't find jobs, we went on welfare. I hated that demeaning process. All the cooking habits and experiences kicked in. I began a small food business. I would cook *barbacoa de cabeza*, not in a *pozo*, but in other people's ovens. My wife Luz would make dozens of flour tortillas. We would buy the corn tortillas. I would make tamales and fajitas at night. By early morning, Luz, Adrián and Tozi, the oldest children, would sell these delicacies as tacos to Mexican workers at various plants and factories. We bought a tamale-making machine in San Antonio before we left for Oregon in 1981. We used to crank out tamales by the hundreds of dozens in a few hours. When the taco business grew beyond the capacity of our home kitchen, I moved some operations to a small room next to the kitchen and also started cooking in our garage. The rainy weather often doesn't permit cooking outdoors in Oregon. The summers are gorgeous in that area of the country, but summer lasts only a month or so. The other three seasons are rain, rain, and rain. The entire coastal area north of San Francisco, California, to Juneau, Alaska, is wet, green, and with permanent air-conditioning, the temperature usually fluctuates between a brisk 50 degrees to 75 degrees Fahrenheit.

When it rained I would cook anyway, with the garage door open, away from the rain and constant drizzle. I even cooked on the day it snowed. A rare occurrence in the coastal Northwest, usually the water comes down as water, not frozen. Somebody called the local television station about my strange behavior. The camera crews came out and filmed me: a crazy Mexican cooking out, barbequing and grilling underneath the overhang of a garage. I was cooking fajitas, *tripitas* and chicken. They just thought that was a funny scene, a real human-interest story. Besides, they were intrigued about the meat being grilled. They had lots of questions that I wouldn't answer outright. I couldn't. To answer completely and honestly would ruin our family business.

Upon our arrival in Oregon, my son Olin, age four, and I lived in Tualatin, a suburb of Portland. Then when Luz, the kids and my mother arrived, we moved to apartments and then a rented home in the foothills of West Salem, the capital city. After I left my job teaching at Colegio César Chávez in Mt. Angel and before I started teaching at Western Oregon State University, we moved to Independence. The local butchers and meat market operators would not sell beef or pig heads, beef skirts (fajitas), glands (*mollejas*) or intestines (*tripas*) to the public. They often throw away these products unless someone asked for them. Customers had to make a special request for them and say it was for dog food, while they bought a few bones to make the order more real. I would buy ten heads, thirty pounds of fajitas or fifty pounds of tripe at a time. The butchers would ask if I was a dog breeder or had lots of dogs. I would say that I froze the meat because I didn't want to come in that often. I rotated meat markets to not make myself obvious. I could not believe they threw away these delicacies before I began to ask for them. By the time I left Oregon in 1986, fajitas were the rage and sold just as expensively as in Texas.

Taking the kids and now the grandkids camping, I've had to teach them how to cook outdoors. When we go to Glendo Lake, Wyoming; Hart Ranch, South Dakota; Bend and Crater Lake, Oregon, or Garner State Park, Texas, cooking is part of the adventure, from planning the meals to dividing the labor of food preparation and the cooking. I wanted to buy property in Bend, Oregon, because you can see Mt. Bachelor, a beautiful snow-capped mountain, nearby. Giant pine trees are everywhere, and the sun shines consistently. Bend is located near the center of the state, away from the coast and the Cascade Mountain Range.

Tozi got real sick in Bend once when we were out camping. I was about to negotiate a land deal, but we had to leave and find a doctor for her. I did not buy that property, but I still have memories of that. I have forever fantasized about working winters in Texas and working summers in Oregon.

The first time I went to Crater Lake, Oregon, was in 1985. We almost drowned. We flipped over in a sailboat. The water in Oregon's lakes, streams, rivers and the ocean is freezing cold. Hypothermia can get you in minutes in the ocean, and in a lake, it takes a bit longer, but it can happen. Fortunately, my mother and my wife insisted that I not take the younger children, Tozi, Olin, and Avina, out on the sailboat. Bob Wilkie, a campus minister at Western Oregon State University, Adrian, my oldest son and I went sailing in Wilkie's boat. Wilkie took his dog with him on the boat. The wind was stiff and constant. We attained good speed as we tacked this way and that, which is how you sail. As the wind catches the sail, the pole holding it whips around from one side to another. Sailors must avoid the sail boom by ducking. Adrian and Wilkie began horsing around, trying to make the boat skim the water by leaning over as far as possible. With their butts hanging over the edge, the water would spray up as they skimmed it. Without warning on one run, they leaned over too much as the boom whipped around, causing the boat to tip over enough to rush water into the boat. We flipped over. Under water I frantically tried to get away from all the ropes and the sail. I lost Adrian. I lost Wilkie. They did not surface. I dove deep and swam under the boat and found them. They both were entangled in ropes and gasping for air. The air bubble under the boat was sufficient but not for long. The rudder disengaged and rose to the surface. Wilkie's dog was barking somewhere outside the capsized boat. I untangled them and tried to convince them to swim down and up around the boat. I assured them that outside was a better place to be and we could grab the boat for buoyancy until help came. They didn't want to leave the security of the air bubble. But I knew it was a matter of minutes before the entire boat would begin to sink, once the air bubble expired. I pulled Adrian out with me. The barking of Wilkie's dog is probably what made Wilkie follow me out. We hung on to the edge of the boat until a rescue boat came out. People on shore saw the incident and promptly called for help, thank goodness. Wilkie hadn't told me that he had had a heart attack just months earlier. He could have died out there in that freezing water. So could we. I'm glad the other kids stayed on shore. My mother scolded me for days and refused to talk to me a few more. Grown men do make mistakes of judgment and prudence.

We went out to Crater Lake again in 1998. I wanted my second wife, Gloria, and her daughter, Lina, as well as our newer little ones to see this beautiful spot of the world. It was another horrible experience. Mosquitoes galore this time, not water. We arrived and set up camp in a great location. Two tents were put up in minutes. I began a fire and pulled meats from the ice chest. The first mosquitoes found us. I thought it was too cold for mosquitoes, but I was wrong. The first ones that found us must have sent word, because reinforcements came. Thousands of mosquitoes attacked us. They were so thick in numbers that they got into your mouth with every breath. We were being eaten up alive. I dropped the meat in my hand on the grill, the girls scampered out of their tents, Gloria dropped the firewood and all of us ran into the Dodge conversion van we owned at the time.

First, we killed all the mosquitoes inside the van. Then, we passed the Calamine lotion around. We were covered with welts. Lina and Andrea are particularly sensitive to mosquitoes and other bug bites. They swell up and hurt and also itch with every bite. Then it started to rain, then to hail, then to rain, and as soon as that storm stopped, I went to check on the condition of the smoldering fire and half-burned meat. The girls and Gloria emerged to see how wet the bedding in the tents had gotten. They had left the entry flaps open when they fled the first mosquito attack. The situation was hopeless, and we began to discuss our options, when the second attack came. The mosquitoes came back with a vengeance. Again, we ran into the van for protection. Again, we killed those in the van and applied more Calamine lotion and Aloe Vera cream to every exposed part of our bodies that had been bitten. We had bites even where we had clothing covering us. I have never had such an experience with mosquitoes that big and that hungry. I've never wanted to go back to Crater Lake, since then.

Now as a grown man, I have taken cooking classes. During my world travels, I have learned to appreciate other foods, such as Italian, French, Spanish, Chinese, and Indian. I've been to Paris, France, and marveled at how they make croissants and delicate sauces. The French use tons of butter in everything. In Barcelona, Spain I've eaten *paella*. This is a fantastic seafood dish of squid, shrimp, clams, crab, lobster and scallops with chicken, pork sausage, rice and peas, all mixed together. The saffron that is used makes the rice a bright yellow-orange. *Sangría*, a red wine and fresh fruit concoction, is served with *paella*.

I've eaten delicious Indian curries, Thai soups, Chinese dim sum, Italian sausage and pasta, and Brazilian and Argentinean *churrascadas*, a red-meat-lovers paradise. I am beginning to learn how to cook those dishes. I will continue to do that. And I will perfect and expand my menu for Mexican food. I cook a delicious *ceviche,* seafood mixture, with lemon juice, cilantro, hot peppers, tomato sauce, and make various *caldos de mariscos,* as well as *pollo en mole, puerco con calabaza,* lamb riblets, and leg of lamb. Food has taught me a lot about myself and other cultures.

Professor and Lawyer

I didn't start college with the goal of becoming a doctor or a lawyer. It was pretty clear to me at an early age that I did not want to be a medical doctor, like my father. We lived in the same building as his medical clinic and laboratory. A mere door separated his office complex from our living quarters. I was always listening to people screaming out in pain, saw him working with blood and once had to help my dad deliver a baby on the sofa in our living room. Patients were always complaining about this pain, that hurt, this injury, that bone, and countless other ills. I saw firsthand and up close the effects of poverty and lack of money among Mexicans in Crystal City. Most of the kids brought to my dad with illness also suffered from malnutrition. Patients usually came to my dad when it was too late. Most poor people wait until the last minute to consult a doctor because they have no money. By the time they see a doctor, there is little a doctor can do. Grown Mexican men are the worst to treat because they never admit to hurt, pain, illness or general malaise, much less depression or loneliness. They are too macho for those admissions. They just live with it, and that is worse oftentimes because they cope or seek a cure with alcohol, drugs, violence and other similar destructive behavior.

Regularly I heard and saw my dad get awakened in the middle of the night to attend to an emergency. He would stay up until all hours of the night with patients. Many of the farmers and growers in the area would just dump people on our sidewalk when they got injured at work. The police would often call my dad and say they were bringing over a badly hurt prisoner. My dad would always complain that the police did the injuries: beatings, concussions, cuts and even gunshots. He often said that to my mother and me, but I suppose he couldn't prove it.

I remembered all of what he went through. I didn't know what I wanted to be when I grew up, but I knew I didn't want to be a doctor. My dad had attended medical school in Torreón, Coahuila, Mexico, but was trained as a doctor during the Mexican Revolution of 1910. Pancho Villa was the first modern-day general to create an ambulatory medical corps. That is, he had young doctors on railroad cars treating his soldiers and horses. My father told me that Villa had a half-brother, Miguel Fernán, who lived in Torreón. Dad thought that Villa was an illegitimate son of Micaela Arámbula and Luis Fernán Gurrola, and not the son of Agustín Arango. Villa's birth certificate, however, recorded his name as José Doroteo Arango. During his early years he took the alias Francisco "Pancho" Villa, and eventually legally changed his name to that.

During a visit to Torreón, Villa learned of the medical school. Villa needed doctors to treat his wounded and sick. He took all the medical students forcibly to Chihuahua with him. During the early years of the revolution, Villa would travel during the night on trains loaded with horses, soldiers, and young doctors. At dawn, wherever he was in the heart of Mexico, he would launch an attack. After the battle, Villa's troops would pick up their dead and wounded, including horses. With everyone back on the train, Villa headed north to Chihuahua. The enemy never knew how much hurt they had inflicted on Villa because there were no bodies. There was nothing but telltale signs of blood and body parts on the battlefields, but no casualties. The doctors on the train ride home tended to the wounded, examined the dead and did what they could for the horses. Horses and humans were the patients. That's where my dad learned how to be a doctor, on the job.

When Villa took Torreón a second time, he declared martial law and left my dad in charge. My dad must have endeared himself to Villa to be given that post. After ten years in the revolution, Villa retired to his ranch in Chihuahua, but was assassinated on July 20, 1923. My dad remained in Torreón. Elections were held in Torreón and my dad was elected mayor, presidente municipal. I have a newspaper article from Torreón's El Demócrata dated September 25, 1925, with my father's picture and the caption, "*Señor Doctor A. Gutiérrez Presidente Municipal.*" He must have been well-liked to be elected. My father, as *presidente municipal*, built many government buildings and paved many streets during his tenure. He bought a building to house his medical practice and his family, my grandmother, Marcelina Crespo de Gutiérrez, and my half-brother, Horacio. I was too young to help my mother fight my half-brother's attempts to take all the property and money from us after my dad died. Horacio stole it all by forging my dad's signature and creating a bogus will. My mother didn't have the money or connections in Mexico to fight him. Horacio took everything except the property in Crystal City. We didn't get a thing from the Mexican holdings. We went into poverty.

While I didn't want to be a doctor, I had to aspire a profession. It was almost like a foregone conclusion that I was going to go to college and become a professional. So I invented an answer to the proverbial questions, "What do you want to be when you grow up? A doctor like your father?" I began to say, "I want to be a lawyer." I don't know where that came from. I had never met a lawyer. As soon as I learned to say, "I want to be a lawyer," that stopped the questions. And it stopped my dad saying, "My son will be a good doctor." I grew up saying I wanted to be a lawyer.

There were a couple of lawyers in town, but they were Anglos, and I had never met them. I didn't know anything about them. I met them after my father died. At age fourteen my mother took me to the county judge, who in turn took me before the district judge to remove my disabilities of minority, a legal proceeding to permit a minor child the privileges of adulthood, such as getting a driver's license or signing a contract. I had to drive myself and conduct my own business legally before I was eighteen years of age. My mother was out of the state most of the time because of better work opportunities. I had to take care of things at home and help my grandmother. We had a little farm where my grandmother lived. We owned our house, and I had to drive myself here and there, to school and work.

While in high school, no one counseled me on which courses to take at college. Once, I was placed in a high school vocational course, woodworking or metal shop, I don't recall. But I protested and was reassigned. On my own I took physics, chemistry, algebra, and geometry. I did that because my other Chicano buddies were taking those courses. And again, we wanted to show Anglo students we could take those courses and beat them on grades. We did. I think we were the first group of Chicano students to track ourselves into a college preparatory curriculum. It was a lot of fun to challenge Anglo students and each other in school. I remember being selected for the National Honor Society in high school. I had no information about financial aid or even how to fill out an application for college admission. Had I been given some advice, I probably would have gone to the University of Texas at Austin (UT) instead of Southwest Texas Junior College in Uvalde. Innocently, I entered my mother's address in Chicago, where she was at the time, on the admission application to UT. I was classified as an out-of-state resident and charged very high nonresident tuition as a result. Several teachers and business people in my hometown wrote letters to the university stating that I was a Crystal City resident and had merely made an honest mistake. The admission personnel were not moved by those letters and refused to change my classification. I could not afford to enroll. I didn't have any grants, loans or scholarships. I missed out on the only scholarship I knew about, a two-hundred-dollar scholarship from the local Mexican Chamber of Commerce. They awarded the scholarship to my classmate, Mike Treviño, the quarterback and captain of our football team. Now, he's a postal clerk in San Antonio. I had to pay my college tuition out of my pocket and could only afford the junior college nearby. Also, had to work as a migrant during the summer months and take other odd jobs in town. During high school, I worked at the J.C. Penney store as a stock boy. While at the junior college, I managed a gas station.

When I graduated from A&I, I sought admission to law school in Houston. Prospective law students and graduate students have to take examinations for admission. I did well on the Law School Admissions Test (LSAT), which supposedly indicated I was going to become a great attorney, very able, very competent. I also took the Graduate Record Examination (GRE) and did poorly, which meant that I wasn't going to do well in an advanced, academic setting. As it turned out, I didn't finish my first round of law school. I had to go a second time when I was forty-one years of age. And I see myself as a mediocre, average lawyer. There's nothing fantastic about my legal ability. On the academic side, I became a professor, an academic, before I became a lawyer. I enjoy academic work and scholarship much more than I do the legal work and trial advocacy. Examinations, such as the LSAT and GRE, are not reliable predictors of professional success, much less enjoyment in what you are really suited for.

While in law school in 1966 to 1967, I lived in the Cougar Apartments and worked full time at the local gas company downtown. I was a credit manager for Houston Natural Gas Company. I approved credit applications for gas air-conditioning. That was good money because I had a college degree, was bilingual, and enrolled in law school. I was an important young executive for a while.

I did not like the study of law at the University of Houston. First, the law school was segregated. There were no women, no black students and only three Chicano students in my freshman class. The student body was a sea of white male faces, mostly from East Texas. I thought the white boys from my part of Texas were bigots, but these outdid them. Too many of them were bigoted rednecks. They were in the process of becoming bigoted redneck lawyers. I hated the thought. Everyday, I had to be prepared to answer the criticisms of my professors and my student peers. Every time I opened my mouth, I seemed to be on the wrong side of the issue. Both students and professors would jump on me and chastise me. I could not keep up with the reading and the stress of extra preparation for each class. I would stay up late trying to do the reading, but I worked full time. I was always sleepy and tired and hungry.

The second disgusting problem with law school was the study of law. I had to read lots and lots of cases to find the theory of law, the issue, the fact pattern, and the appellate history. Every professor would call on students to answer questions. We had to stand and respond with the correct answer. Ultimately, the most used answer in law school to any question was precedent or *stare decisi*. That's a fancy way of saying "because we already said so." The judges on the highest courts in the country ultimately decide important cases on first impressions. That becomes the law. Cases similar to those are decided by applying that decision, the rule of law. New cases are decided by old cases. Anglo-Saxon common law is just that. It's decisions that were reached as they went along over the years. I would get in trouble when I said that they made these up to justify theft, plunder, and corruption. That is what I read between the lines when I read the cases. For example, when land is stolen and held by the thief for a number of years, it becomes his or hers. It's called adverse possession. If a buyer pays for stolen property, he or she keeps it if they did not know it was stolen. A bona fide purchaser, the buyer is called. How convenient! To me, theft is theft. How can someone claim to have discovered a mineral, land, object or other resource like salt or sand, put a fence around it, and claim it is theirs? What gives that process a superior right over the inhabitants already there? Anglo-Saxon common law is the answer. Native Americans' rights of nations and sovereignty, Spanish law, French law, Mexican law are not valid. Those who win write the laws and history books. Land grants made to past ancestors and communal lands of Indian nations are invalid. Title to land is recognized only if it is conveyed how the present system dictates and the papers are recorded in the courthouse. They must be in English. Except in New Mexico, where the official languages are both Spanish and English. I got tired of arguing constantly. It became pointless. I did not matter. My analyses and opinions were wrong. Theirs were right because of eight hundred years of Anglo-Saxon common law.

Lastly, there wasn't very much intellectual challenge in the study of law. You read the cases and black letter law, you outlined, memorized, recalled, and applied those principles to the facts of the case on an exam. One exam at the end of the semester determined your final grade.

I also didn't like the location and environment of the University of Houston Bates College of Law. It was in the basement of E. Cullen Performance Hall on the main campus off Elgin, Calhoun and Scott Streets, the same building where Arte Público Press now is housed.

I couldn't see myself going to school with these professional rednecks-in-the-making or practicing law out in that part of the state. I knew from having talked to Jesse Gámez and Ambrosio Meléndez that St. Mary's University Law School in San Antonio, like Bates College of Law, were regional law schools. Jesse and Ambrosio were enrolled in St. Mary's Law School. If you graduated from St. Mary's Law School, you probably were going to practice in South Texas. If you graduated from Thurgood Marshall Law School at Texas Southern University, the historic black law school also in Houston, you probably were going to practice in the Rio Grande Valley of South Texas. If you went to Bates, where I was, you probably were going to stay and practice in Houston or East Texas. If you graduated from UT-Austin Law School, where everybody tried to enroll, then you probably would practice wherever you wanted. The big law firms seek these graduates before others. UT-Austin law grads are connected to a lot of people. The flagship schools, UT-Austin, as all the other Texas public universities, only admit 10 percent non-Texans. These public schools are for Texas residents.

Lubbock had a reputation for an oil and gas specialty in that law school. I was not interested in oil and gas. I was not interested in Baylor Law School and its tight Baptist atmosphere. Those were the law schools I knew I could transfer to from Houston. I had had a bad experience with UT-Austin. I didn't want to attend Texas Southern University's law school. I did not see myself going to practice in the Rio Grande Valley. I wanted to return to Crystal City, maybe San Antonio, but I couldn't afford St. Mary's University's tuition. I didn't want to be a lawyer anymore. I decided to quit law school. My academic mentor, Charlie Cotrell, formerly at Texas A&I, invited me to graduate school at St. Mary's in San Antonio. He was teaching there as was Bill Crane, whom I had met during the 1963 elections in Crystal City. Charlie promised me a job as proctor and some work-study to help pay the tuition. I accepted readily. I wanted to pursue the academic side now. I resigned from the gas company, left my apartment to the roommates, sold my law books, and moved during the Christmas holidays to San Antonio. I lived with Charlie and his wife Glenda for about a month until I found housing. My mother had divorced her second husband, Oscar, and moved in with me. She helped pay the rent and utilities. I also didn't have to cook, wash clothes or iron. Mother did that for me once again.

My job as proctor at St. Mary's basically had me administering and grading freshman-level exams and papers. Occasionally I would call the class roll and make announcements about assignments or class activities, and sometimes I'd tutor students. For Dr. Cotrell and Crane and other professors, I managed the outside reading assignments. I checked out books for the professor and placed books and articles on reserve for student reading.

My first graduate courses in government and history were tremendous. It was like intellectual heaven had opened up. When I would ask a question in these classes, instead of hearing "because of eight hundred years of Anglo-Saxon common law," I heard, "Well, why don't you read these three articles and check out these four books?" It was like swimming in a world of ideas. All of a sudden, there was no right or wrong, and there was no memorizing this rule or that black-letter law. It was many theories and concepts and trends among and within the different schools of thought. I fell in love with the intellectual stimulus. The jargon of frameworks, models, paradigms and analyses was so new and refreshing. The very idea that there was no right or wrong answer, but many answers, was fascinating. I found that I could incorporate lawyering skills in these courses. I researched the evidence, presented an argument, defended my points with citations to research and added as much passion to the delivery as necessary. I could combine written arguments from theories with my experiences. I was validated in my prior political activities. Participant observation, personal interviews, and windshield survey research was valid. My opinions were not dismissed as "out of hand" in graduate school. On the contrary, the fact that I had been involved in real electoral activity in college and community environments made me somewhat of an expert. When called upon to discuss a question or issue, I felt knowledgable. My confidence and happiness grew with every course and every semester. I was able to combine the best of both worlds, legal and academic. I've always been a good debater and conversationalist, particularly in persuasive argument and advocacy. In this academic setting, I was now using the skills I learned as a social activist and law school student to press for my intellectual pursuits. I loved every minute of reading, research, writing and class discussion. I knew I was headed toward a doctoral degree from the first days at St. Mary's University.

I traded roommates in the middle of my master's program: my mother for Luz Bazán. I asked Luz to marry me. She had been my favorite girlfriend while I attended A&I in Kingsville. I never adjusted to dating Anglo and black girls in Houston. I felt comfortable with Luz because we had a lot in common, including visions. She moved to San Antonio and began teaching. We were married on July 15, 1967. I continued to zip through my master's degree and wrote a provocative thesis about the conditions for revolution in four South Texas counties, Zavala County, my home turf, was one of them. I compared these counties and South Texas to stable dictatorships across the world, particularly in Mexico and Latin America. I made the argument that Chicanos still were colonial subjects. Colonization had implications for the way we saw the world, our role in it, and how the world saw us. The social, political, and economic dichotomy unfolded as we were subtracted from the world as human beings while being re-made into an Anglo image. The Anglos call the process assimilation; we learned to be like them. It does not occur to them that we do not want to become Anglos, that we are perfectly happy the way we are. I called assimilation a process of subtraction; we don't get to be ourselves. The few that become Anglo-like are the 10 percent that turn against us. The remaining 90 percent that don't quite assimilate then become the underclass workers: garbage collectors, farmworkers, dishwashers, maids, gardeners, roofers and criminals, the service class. We then become the understratum of white society. This status is perfectly acceptable to Anglos because someone has got to do those jobs, but not them. It used to be blacks, now it is Mexicans. When I wrote this thesis, I didn't think it was all that shocking. It was eye-opening for me, however. Other people thought this was really profound and startling. I realized then the power of words and research. I knew that someday I would have to write books and put my ideas in print. And because of that I've written several books.

When I wasn't in class discussing politics, I was in the student center discussing politics. At St. Mary's, I met Mario Compeán and Willie Velásquez. I already knew Juan Patlán from the junior college days in Uvalde. Ignacio Pérez was brought into our circle. We began to formulate plans for organizing a youth group. We formed the Mexican American Youth Organization (MAYO). I also was writing my thesis. Luz typed it on an old typewriter using carbon paper to make copies. Every time she made a mistake, she had to flip to each copy and erase. There were no personal computers or photocopiers during that time. By the following year, I graduated and Luz was pregnant with our first child. We moved to Austin, and I began my doctoral program in government. I was shocked to learn that at that time I was the only Chicano in the entire state of Texas enrolled in a Ph.D. in government.

During my studies in Austin, both times, I worked full-time and was an activist full time. I have never simply attended school and not worked, except for two opportunities, a Dean's scholarship at UT in 1971 and three postgraduate seminars. Those are the only times that I have just gone to school and enjoyed academic life. I never stopped going to school after that. Today, I threaten that I might go back to medical school or something else that interests me. But the only school I've been going to is cooking school.

Our baby boy, Adrian, was born in Austin at Seaton Hospital. Bill Richey, a former student at A&I and St. Mary's, was in San Marcos studying and drove up. Together, we went to see Luz and the baby; both were doing really well. Then, he and I celebrated the birth of my son with a cookout.

I was working for State Senator Joe Bernal of San Antonio at the time. There was a special legislative session in progress, and he hired me as his legislative assistant. But Ruth Webb, the Selective Service secretary in Uvalde who had a life-passion to draft every Mexican she could identify, got me. Fortunately, I received word ahead of time that my draft notice was being typed and would be in the mail the next day. I immediately drove around South Texas to Corpus Christi, Laredo, San Antonio, Hondo, Houston, and Austin calling and visiting the various Army Reserve Units to look for a vacancy. I found a unit in San Antonio, the 277th Combat Engineers, and signed up. When the draft notice reached me, I was committed to the Army Reserve. They would call me to active duty in a few months and advised me to notify my employer. I was out of a job when the special session ended. We moved to San Antonio, so Luz could return to teaching. I had to abandon my doctoral program for the time being.

During the various MAYO projects, we made a case for a legal defense fund to protect and promote Chicano civil rights. Many lawyers and Chicano politicians, such as Albert Peña, Jr., felt the same way, especially those who worked with us on social protests and demonstrations. We, as MAYO organizers, met with lawyers in Wimberly, Texas, to plan the formation of a legal defense fund. Out of those meetings, our local militancy, and the Chicano Movement across the Southwest, the Mexican American Legal Defense and Education Fund (MALDEF) was established in San Antonio. I was hired as the first civil rights investigator for MALDEF. I didn't present my letter instructing me to report for military duty until the last days.

On October 20, 1968, five days before my birthday, I was on an airplane heading out to Ft. Leonard Wood, Missouri, nestled in the Ozark Mountains. I went to basic training there. I remember arriving with a change of clothes, a T-shirt and khaki pants, plus what I had on. That's all I took. It was freezing at the military base. I made the mistake of washing my underwear in the barracks the first night. They didn't dry. The next day I went around without underwear. We had to run everywhere. I was grimy, dirty, smelly and raw by the end of the day. All of us had to sleep on a plain mattress without sheets. The drill sergeants opened every other window of the barracks for fresh air. I got an open window by my bunk. It was so cold. I folded the mattress and crawled in-between like a sandwich. I was so miserable. Once we got our Army clothes and bedding, things looked up a bit. The food was nasty but plentiful. The coffee was hot and black. I learned to drink it like that and to like it. When I got my Army haircut and all the hair hit the floor, I realized I really had big ears. At Christmastime, I was sent home because we had finished our basic training. They had shortened the training time because more troops were needed in Vietnam. The casualties were mounting, especially Chicanos.

I recall getting off the bus in San Antonio and Luz standing there with the baby in her arms. She didn't recognize me. I walked right past her, and she didn't know it was me, I looked that different. Although my nametag was on my uniform, I was bald and skinny but muscular. I was all ears and head without my moustache. Luz had never seen me like that. I looked like the Jolly Green Giant of the television commercials.

I spent a few days with her and Adrian. He was a joy to play with. He was a big boy for five months of age. We went to Crystal City to see my mother and grandmother. While we were there, I mentioned to people that Luz and I were moving come back to Crystal City as soon as I got out of the military. That announcement is probably what caused some Anglo kids to burn my grandmother's house down. Fortunately, my grandmother was not there at the time of the fire. She was visiting relatives in San Antonio. The house burned to the ground. Later I learned that the local volunteer fire department had responded to the call by coming by to watch it burn down. Not one water hose was turned on. I also heard from people in the neighborhood that two white kids on a motorcycle, one a redhead, were seen going up to the house with a can, then speeding away from the blaze. I found out that the redhead was Jimmy Walker, son of the Walkers who ran the Western Auto franchise in Crystal City. No charges were ever filed against him or anyone.

I was released from the military in April 1969, and it was too late to start the semester at the university. I tried to get my job back at MALDEF, but Pete Tijerina, the director, wouldn't hire me. Henry B. González, the local congressman, was very opposed to anyone who posed a threat to his leadership position. He was adamant that I not be hired. Congressman González always criticized Bexar County Commissioner Albert Peña, Jr., San Antonio Councilman Pete Torres, State Senator Joe Bernal, State Representatives John Alaníz and Rudy Esquivel and MAYO members. We were the young militants he despised. He was always badmouthing us, calling us racists in reverse and Brown Bilbos, after Senator Bilbo from Mississippi, an arch-racist. González was just horrible.

Pete Tijerina told me that if he didn't fire me, MALDEF would lose its funding. I had to go. I threatened Pete right back. I said, "Well, if you let me go, I'll sue you and MALDEF, because all soldiers must get their jobs back as soon as they return from duty. How is that going to look in the newspapers? MALDEF does not believe in civil rights for its employees!" Fortunately, Mario Obledo, the general counsel, interceded and arranged for a settlement. They paid me off. Luz and I and the baby took the money and went traveling. Before we left, we applied for jobs with the Crystal City Independent School District. We both had degrees. I had a master's degree and Luz had almost completed her MA at Trinity University. She was a certified teacher with experience. We dropped off our applications and headed on to New Mexico to spend time with Reies López Tijerina, the leader of the Land Recovery Movement.

Our baby got sick, so we had to leave earlier than expected and find a doctor. The closest clinic was in Espanola, New Mexico. When the baby was better we headed north to Denver to visit the Crusade for Justice and Rodolfo "Corky" Gonzales and then we went to California to visit with César Chávez. We learned firsthand how the Chicano leaders conducted their operations. We spent hours visiting, talking to people, watching what they did and how they did it.

Luz and I knew that upon our return to Crystal City, we would be heading up our own organization and operations. In New Mexico, Tijerina was focused on getting the land back. He was an outstanding public speaker in both Spanish and English. Rodolfo "Corky" Gonzales, on the other hand, was English-speaking, urban, a former boxer. He espoused community control. His organization, the Crusade for Justice, would take control of public parks and set up a new Chicano governing council with rules. To me this was the same thing as taking the land back, except these locations were parks and areas in the city. César Chávez, on the other hand, bought his own land, forty acres, near Keene, California. They called this farmworker headquarters La Paz. They owned their own phone company, health clinic, housing, cafeteria, credit union, printing press, and theatre group. They had everything. They were self-contained.

I began to formulate an idea of what Aztlán should be once we were able to do this. Luz was my echo. But it was very premature. We were just picking up ideas on how these men led these movements. *Aztlán* was the Aztec name for the original land they occupied in present-day Utah before the tribe made its pilgrimage in search of the promised land, where an eagle with a snake in its beak perched on a cactus would appear. That is Mexico City.

When we returned to Crystal City, we didn't have jobs. We had little money, but no jobs. Victoriano "Nano" Serna started helping us print a newspaper, La Verdad. He basically paid for its printing until we began to get advertisements. He gave me hamburgers and a case of beer for organizing. The Chicano culture in Crystal City was very traditional. Luz had to work with the women, and I with the men. We wrote a proposal to fund a migrant mobile Head Start program that would follow migrant kids during the summer months. We got it funded. We hooked up with Luis Díaz de León and the Colorado Migrant Council to manage the grant. That became a very successful program. We became the directors of the Head Start programs in the Winter Garden area. Today, it's called the Texas Migrant Council, and it is based in Laredo, Texas. It has received millions of dollars for migrant education.

Education pays off in a big way. Being able to write well and follow directions is very important. We became tremendous grant writers, and large amounts of federal and foundation money poured into Crystal City. For example, Luz wrote the grant with help from some people in Michigan for a health clinic in Crystal City. A lot of programs were developed because of our academic backgrounds and abilities. We taught others how to write proposals and grant applications.

If a person only gets a high school diploma or a GED, they are doomed to a life of poverty. They can expect to earn about a million dollars in their lifetime. That is not much when you divide the number of years a person lives on the average. The only exceptions are high school graduates who get a government job with benefits that includes a pension after twenty years of service. The pension is not going to be worth much, and you'll still need supplementary income. Working and relying on Social Security is not enough—a person can't survive. If a person graduates from college, she or he will earn about three to five million dollars in their lifetime. A professional degree, such as lawyer, architect, engineer or doctor, for example, will earn five million dollars or more in an average lifetime. The sky is the limit in the lifetime of a professional person. That amount of money is real wealth. A professional person can leave an inheritance of money and property to heirs from then on. Children can get an economic head start in life with that wealth. Poor children have to start all over again, just like their parents, and most do not make it out of poverty. Poverty breeds poverty. College education breeds college education. The first to reach a college degree is the first to begin an upward spiral toward better health, housing, income, recreation, cars, jobs, and success for their families and subsequent generations. There are college graduates who mess up, but almost everybody is going to be better off after the first one that goes to college.

It was always clear to me that all of my kids were going to go to college and be better off. That is the way we should all think. That's the way we all thought during the Chicano Movement era.

The people I meet now from those times have all gone to college, done well, and their kids are doing very well. In fact, it may be that we've done so well that their kids now are not Chicanos. They call themselves Hispanics and Latinos. They have no clue what price our generation paid to get this far. More importantly, today most young people of Mexican ancestry were not born in the United States and were born after the Chicano Movement. They have no clue what my generation was about or did.

I never stopped going to school. I registered again for a Ph.D. program in 1971 after the Crystal City success with the Raza Unida Party and elections. I would get up at 3:30 A.M. and drive to Austin, about a three-hour drive. I would sit in classes all day Tuesday and Wednesday, and Thursday evening drive home. I slept on an army cot in an apartment rented by the Rodríguez brothers from the Rio Grande Valley. I would do my political work on Friday, Saturday, Sunday and Monday. One weekend every month, I would have to go to my Army Reserve meeting in San Antonio. I kept that schedule for a number of years until we moved to San Antonio in 1972, so that Luz could complete her MA at Trinity University. I was awarded a dean's scholarship from Dean Stanley Ross while I completed course work for my Ph.D. Dr. Américo Paredes, the director of the doctoral program in which I was teaching, and I had a discussion about this money. He announced to me one day that I would receive this scholarship if I stopped pursuing my Ph.D. program full time. All I had to do was stop teaching. I was teaching a Chicano politics class at UT. The dean wanted me out of the classroom. He didn't want me expounding my ideas in the classroom to hundreds of students. I would lecture with a microphone in this giant auditorium. I had two people help me with attendance, grading, passing out materials, and administering exams. When the offer of the scholarship was made, I jumped at the money. I was so tired of the driving, working, studying, and looking for money to make ends meet.

Dr. Paredes didn't tell me about his conversation with Dean Ross. I don't think he knew my situation either. But he did say to me, "Why are you getting out of the classroom? Just for the money?" And I said, "Yes. I need it. I have a growing family. I've got two kids and maybe another on the way." Olin was about to be born. Américo was very disappointed that I took the scholarship. But I did. I was better off for it because I had more money for my family and politics. Politics takes a lot of money. I was paying my own phone bill for calls made on behalf of the Raza Unida Party. In many ways, I was the Raza Unida Party. The telephone bill would be three to four hundred dollars a month, which was a lot of money in the seventies. Our gasoline bills were high, another three to four hundred dollars a month. We were expending a lot of money in keeping up with the movement and its activities.

What I didn't know at the time was that university authorities, Dean Stanley Ross among them, were trying to get me out of the classroom at the request of the Federal Bureau of Investigation (FBI). When we began a Freedom of Information Act investigation and systematically requested government documents (mostly FBI documents) about the Raza Unida Party and its activists, I found out the FBI had visited Dean Ross and asked that I be removed from the classroom. The FBI knew I needed money. Dr. Paredes did not.

We bought our first home in San Antonio during this time. We lived part-time in Crystal City, part-time in San Antonio, and although we were part-timers at the universities, we enrolled with full course loads. We continued the organizing and operation of the Raza Unida Party. We sought and obtained statewide ballot status in 1972.

I traveled a lot, giving speeches and making money as a consultant. When you have a degree and you have something to say, people will pay you good dollars to listen to your words and to read them. It's a very good life. I finished my course work for my Ph.D. in 1975 and began writing my dissertation. I was awarded the degree in 1976. A chapter in my dissertation caused a lot of problems. The graduate supervising committee wouldn't accept it. I was criticized for not using enough primary sources and not employing the accepted jargon of the discipline. I didn't have enough footnotes, but I did have personal observation and anecdotal evidence.

Well, I couldn't have other sources. This was cutting-edge material. No one had ever written about power relations between Anglos and Mexicans. How could I be expected to cite sources that did not exist at that particular time? Books and articles on Chicano politics were beginning to be published. I moved the controversial chapter to the end of the dissertation and called it an Appendix.

My dissertation never has been published, but the Appendix has. That became my first book to be published on a large scale, *A Gringo Manual on How to Handle Mexicans*. My paperback book was self-published in Mexico. It was the first bilingual, self-help book about power relations for Chicanos. Mine was a very pioneering effort. U.S. academic presses had rejected it, saying it was racist in reverse, that I was a bitter man, that I was too angry, and that it was subversive. I thought it was humorous and funny. At that time it was quite a provocative book, and so I had to print it in Mexico, where printing was cheaper. I was able to print twenty thousand copies. When I tried to cross them into Texas from Piedras Negras, Coahuila, U.S. Customs authorities deemed the book subversive material. They wanted to confiscate all the copies. I turned around and drove back into Mexico. I had the books smuggled across the border and have been selling them ever since, of course now in subsequent editions.

I finished my Ph.D. in 1976 and began teaching at the college level. I remember teaching courses for Our Lady of the Lake and then Chicago State and San Diego State universities. These universities offered courses in Crystal City.

I finished my term on the school board in 1973 and ran for county judge under the Raza Unida Party in Zavala County and won. I won twice in fact, in 1974 and in 1978. County judges in Texas do not have to be lawyers, but it helps. I had lawyers practicing in front of me as the judge. They argued their cases, and I would rule on their objections, points of evidence, and motions. I prepared jury charges in civil cases and assessed punishment in criminal and juvenile cases. I was acting like a lawyer. I decided I was going to go back to law school, but I wasn't able to. We ended up having to leave Crystal City when the county commissioners lowered my salary.

I went in search of consultant contracts and ultimately began teaching full time at the Colegio César Chávez in Mt. Angel, Oregon, then later at Western Oregon State University. I earned tenure and a promotion to associate professor in 1985. The Department of Social Sciences gave me tenure the fifth year of teaching. Because the Oregon economy was in a tailspin, there were layoffs in higher education. I got cut on the fifth round.

I took a job with United Way in Portland, Oregon. They were looking for someone who could organize emerging populations of Mexicans and Vietnamese in the metropolitan area. I got the position and did a bang-up job, especially for Hispanics. I organized an annual conference on the state of Hispanics in Oregon and published a book of issues. I organized the Oregon Council for Hispanic Advancement and started a leadership program for Chicano youth. It's still funded and operating in Salem, the capital. I organized the Northwest Voter Education and Registration Project and obtained funding for the Hispanic Commission by renaming it, with legislative approval, the Governor's Commission on Hispanic Affairs. The governor provided money to start the programs. I became the executive director of that agency. I was working and traveling too much, I was too involved in state politics. So was Luz. She was heading a health clinic in Woodburn, Oregon, and was involved with a new organization she and María Viramontes Marín had formed, Mujeres de Oregon. We did not have time for each other, and we did not have the Chicano Movement to keep us together. Our children were growing, and that was all we had in common. My marriage to Luz ended in 1985. I moved out and moved back in, but it was of no use. We got divorced.

I had my Ph.D. but it was of little value in Oregon. There were no jobs in higher education. I always wanted to return to law school and become a lawyer. I am the kind of person who just doesn't quit on ideas and goals. I applied for admission at Willamette Law School in Salem and was awarded a full scholarship. Who knows what would have happened if I had stayed there. Willamette University is a private school attended by lots of people in Oregon. My guess is that I probably would have stayed in the Northwest and become a great lawyer or judge. There were very few Spanish-speaking practicing lawyers in Oregon in 1986. Bobby Gutiérrez was a lawyer, but he worked for the president of Oregon State University and Judge Joseph Ceniceros was in Portland. There really weren't any practicing attorneys that I knew of who were Spanish-speaking.

About the same time, I read an advertisement in the local newspaper for a job in Texas with a legal foundation. The Texas Rural Legal Foundation needed an executive director to manage the caseload and monies. I applied and was chosen. I came back to Texas. In Dallas, I met with Domingo García and Roberto Alonzo, who were planning on opening a law firm. They asked me to join them when I finished law school. I applied for admission to the law school at Southern Methodist University and was accepted. I received half a scholarship, but their tuition rates were so expensive that I had to transfer to the University of Houston Bates College of Law. I was back where I had started twenty years earlier. I graduated from law school in 1988 and became a lawyer. I also got married again in 1988, to Gloria Garza from Mission, Texas. She had been a teacher in Crystal City during the 1970s.

I returned to Dallas with a wife and a new child, Andrea. Actually, we had two girls, because Gloria had Lina from a prior marriage. I joined the García, Alonzo, García and Gutiérrez law firm and we opened offices at 1005 W. Jefferson in Oak Cliff, deep in the heart of a large Mexican community in Dallas. I became the managing partner for the firm and handled my own caseload. A lawyer can make a lot of money if he or she has money to start with, because cases require an investment of capital. Witnesses, especially expert witnesses, are very expensive and vital to a case. Support staff is also expensive. It is not easy to maintain an office. Advertising is very expensive. If a lawyer gets a moneymaking case early in his/her career, he or she can leverage that money into bigger and more complex cases. The opposite is also true. If the beginning lawyer does not get a moneymaking case, he or she has to spend their time making ends meet and not moving up to handle more complex cases that pay well. Cash-starved lawyers must refer their good cases to other attorneys and earn less than the full amount. They cannot easily get out of that rut. And not all cases make money. There are three kinds of cases: Cases with good facts and terrible clients, cases with terrible facts and great clients, and then, the ultimate moneymaking case, which is great facts and a great client. With a case like that, lawyers want to go to court, because the client and the lawyer are both going to go to the bank smiling. But you've got to hang onto your money after a good case; otherwise you can't finance your cases later on. Most lawyers can't do that, so they never rise to the top. They fall into a niche and all they do are divorces or juvenile and criminal cases or immigration work, and they stay there. Super lawyers eventually advance because they are able to leverage their money and finance a big case.

I'd been a judge before and, with a law degree, I was selected as one of the first Chicano administrative law judges for the city of Dallas. I held that position for a couple of years and could have moved on to become a municipal judge. I still can. I've now been a lawyer for more than ten years, which is the average number of years required for judicial eligibility. I can basically practice in any state. I've done some federal cases in Arizona and Texas and in Washington, D.C.'s Court of Claims. I've been to the U.S. Supreme Court on a case, *LULAC versus Mattox*, a redistricting case involving the election of district judges from single-member districts. I could easily go in many directions, but now I'm tired of lawyering.

I'm hoping that maybe one of my children or my son-in-law, Juan Tijerina, will succeed me. Olin and Juan are both studying law. Clavel, my youngest daughter, says she is going to be a lawyer. Tozi, my oldest daughter, still says she wants to study law. Tozi has worked in my law office before and knows the workings of the law. She pursued social work and executive administrative work and has made good money with her master's degree. I've helped her sue some employers who hurt her. We sued State Farm Insurance and the Hidalgo County Workforce Commission on her behalf. She has been able to realize good settlement amounts, enough to buy a house in Houston and help her husband's study of law. Lawyering is really good for you. I've been able to build a building, hire lawyers to work for me, and raise a large family. I hope to pass my practice on to one of my children.

I still haven't lost my interest in academics. My love is the academic life. I began as an adjunct faculty member at the University of Texas at Dallas for a year. Then there was a vacancy at UT-Arlington for a person to teach ethnic politics. I was chosen after a national search and I've been there now twelve years. During my third year at this university, I started the Center for Mexican-American Studies (CMAS). State Representative Roberto Alonzo helped me get funding from the legislature. The CMAS program went very, very well until the administration decided that I was too political and wanted to take my funding and staff positions. I was not allowed to resign or end my appointment time and was fired. So I had no choice but to protect my reputation and name. Fortunately, I am a lawyer. I sued them twice and defeated them both times. CMAS is still there and operating on a limited budget, and it has a new director.

Today, I am simply a tenured, full professor teaching and writing books. I have sought other jobs at various universities, such as UT-Pan American, UT-Brownsville, and UT-San Antonio. I would like to teach and work where there are more Mexican-American students. There are not many in Arlington. I have not had success at those three institutions. Committees, student groups, and, community have chosen me as the finalist, but the administration just doesn't follow through. I think that they feel threatened by my presence or they don't want my point of view reflected in their political science departments. I haven't been able to get out of UT-Arlington. It looks like I'm probably going to stay here for now, or until I retire in fifteen years or so. I have learned that being a professor and a lawyer is a tremendous combination.

At one of my birthday parties in Torreón, Coahuila, Mexico.

Grandmother Refugio "Cuca" Fuentes, Aunt Lucía while she attended Ursuline Academy, and I in Laredo, TX.

With javalina in Crystal City outskirts.

With State Senator José Bernal, Special Session in Austin, TX, 1968.

In MAYO National Convention in La Lomita, Mission, TX, December 1969.

Addressing people interested in La Raza Unida Party in Chicago, ILL, 1970.

As County Judge for Zavala County in Texas in 1975.

In Austin, TX, after being sworn in and admitted to the Bar of Texas as an attorney in December 1989.

With my daughters Andre Lucía and Clavel Amariz in Cozumel, Mexico, 2004.

While teaching at Our Lady of the Lake University in San Antonio, TX, on March 5, 2004.

At home in Arlington, TX, on my birthday on October 25, 2004.

Travel

One of the most exciting memories I have of my childhood is traveling. My early recollections of trips date to when I was perhaps seven or eight years old. My dad drove a 1952 Buick. My mother would get all dolled up, smelling pretty, and we would go to Piedras Negras, Coahuila, Mexico, some forty-seven miles from Crystal City, for dinner and other things. Eagle Pass, Texas, was the border town across from Piedras. Everybody I knew just called the town by the first word of the two. My dad would visit his friends, Armando Treviño and Jesús Ismael Rodríguez. The latter became my ophthalmologist and the former the treating physician when my dad died in Piedras Negras.

My mother and I would always go to the *mercado*. The marketplace was a delight. It was called El Parián and occupied an entire city block, just down from the central plaza and the city's cathedral. I remember the aromas: food cooking, fresh flowers, raw meat, ground coffee, ground chocolate, freshly made corn tortillas. The smells depended on what section of the Parián you were in. My mother walked the entire marketplace at least twice, sometimes three times, before she decided on what to buy. At one corner was the *tortillería,* where they made fresh, corn tortillas. You could smell the process from the fresh corn soaking in lime to the *masa* paste being patted into *testales* before rounding them by hand into a tortilla and slapping them on the cooking machine. The warm tortillas were dumped into a big tub. The sales-people would grab the tortillas by the handful and count out your order, then wrap them in brown butcher paper. I loved it when my mother bought tortillas and avocados because that meant that we would eat some on the drive back to Crystal City. The avocados could be brought into the United States, but only if they did not have the pit in them. The vendors would take them out and place a lime in its place. Another corner had cooked food: *atoles, guisos, cabrito, chiles,* and *frijoles*. All of these were served on fresh tortillas. People would sit on stools or just stand eating their *taquitos*. My dad would eventually find us in the *mercado*. If he didn't come for us, we would look for him by walking on the outside of the Parián until we spotted the Buick being washed by a young boy with a pail. I was always amazed that one pail of water would be enough to wash that big car. We would invariably find my dad talking with someone while he smoked his usual Camel cigarette. He knew a lot of people in Piedras.

We would go to the banks across from the *mercado*; there were three. Mexican banks are elegant: marble floors, high ceilings, rich and dark mahogany desks, and lots of people. In the bank were Mexican men in dark suits sitting in offices behind big desks. I did not see that in Crystal City. I was glad to see that there were important Mexicans in Piedras Negras. I associated the wearing of a suit with being important. I had the same thoughts about women. The only pretty women I saw were the Anglo teachers and my mom. Working inside the bank were very many beautiful Mexican women, very well dressed, with pretty jewelry, walking in high heels, and a ready smile if you caught their eye. The women were always walking briskly from one desk to another. Their heels would make a rapid clickety-click, clickety-click when they walked on the marble floors. The prettiest ones sat behind desks in front of the offices with the men. There was always a very pretty lady sitting close to the door from the street. She would stand up as soon as she saw my father or mother and greet them by name. If we were all together, my dad would be escorted promptly to meet with one of the Mexican men in a suit in a big office, and my mother would be walked over to another man at a big desk. Then, I got the full attention of a pretty lady. She would sit me down next to her and offer me something to drink, cookies, and candies. Mexican candies were different. They came unwrapped and were made of pumpkin, watermelon, orange, milk with pecans, and sweet potato. If I asked for a drink, they would bring me a Mexican juice or soft drink in a real glass with a napkin wrapped around it, but no ice.

Behind the large counter with little windows in the middle of the bank lobby sat many more young women who cashed money and made deposits. They also smiled at you when you walked up to them. They all spoke Spanish and had beautiful white, straight teeth. I always wondered where so many beautiful people like that came from—not Crystal City for sure.

My dad and my mom did business at the banks. And then we would end up at either El Moderno, which was the name of a fancy restaurant, or at El Pedegral. El Moderno was at the end of the bridge that crossed into Mexico and it was overlooking the bluff down to the river. It had many windows and you could see Eagle Pass. I loved to stand by the windows and watch the boys below by the riverbank dive into the water to retrieve coins that people driving across the bridge would toss at them. My dad never let me throw money out the window. He said that would only encourage the practice. I did not understand then what he meant. I always thought it was a good practice; the kids below got free money while swimming in the river. When I got a bit older I would throw money out the window, anyway, while my dad was busy driving. Indians used to live down below on the riverbank also. My dad said they were Kickapoo Indians, who had separated from the other Indians in Oklahoma. Some Mexican Kickapoo Indians were black. He explained that Mexico, when it owned Texas, did not allow slavery, and the Kickapoo Indians did not either. African slaves that ran away from white slave owners found refuge with Mexicans and Kickapoos, but when the *gringos* stole Texas, both the Mexicans and the Kickapoos retreated further south into Mexico. They married each other. Texas under *gringo* rule did not allow that kind of marriage either. Dad promised we would visit Músquiz, Coahuila,

Mexico, where black Mexican Kickapoos lived, but we never did. I just read about it later in college. Now, in Eagle Pass, there is no river below the bridge; it is dry for the most part.

In the restaurant, my dad would get upset because I would order a hamburger or fried chicken. He wanted me to eat real Mexican food, as he put it. *Cabrito* or *arracheras,* now called fajitas. But mostly *cabrito* is what he wanted me to eat, and eventually I did develop a taste for it. I love it, and lamb too. I also remember the *guacamole* and refried beans that they would make at the Moderno and the *cajeta* we would have for dessert. It all tasted so good.

Sometimes we would travel to San Antonio. My mother would go shopping at Joske's and we would have lunch right around the corner at the Menger Hotel. I remember that used to be so luxurious to me. It was an elegant hotel. I never saw Mexicans there—except for the waiters, some of the porters that helped with the luggage, and us. We never had luggage, except lots of shopping bags. We just ate there, but did not lodge there. I didn't like the drive to San Antonio because it was too far. It took about two hours. But when we got there and made it into downtown, the tall buildings were a sight to see. I marveled at how they didn't fall down like trees do in a strong wind. The elevators inside these tall buildings were lots of fun, they made your stomach feel funny when they zoomed up and stopped suddenly at the different floors. I could ride those elevators all day.

I didn't do much in San Antonio other than shop with my mother. My father would drop us off and disappear to who knows where. When I asked, he would say he went to visit Don Rómulo Munguía, the Mexican consul, or some of the Mexican pharmacists by the *mercado*. San Antonio also had a *mercado*. It was located on the Mexican side of town by the Santa Rosa Hospital. At the appointed hour, regardless of where he had been, Dad would meet us at the Menger Hotel.

The trips that were also very long, but I enjoyed them because of the danger involved, were to Torreón, where my dad had property. We would drive forever, it seemed to me, and come to a place called La Cuesta de Mambulique, with high mountains, dangerous curves, steep bluffs, and narrow roads. Sometimes we would stop in Monterrey and visit my mom's side of the family. There was a place there that was very pretty, Cola de Caballo, a waterfall. The drive to both places was on the edge of mountains, with lots of twists and turns and ups and downs on the highway. I thought it was just fascinating to experience the risk of danger.

I don't remember much about the specific reasons for trips to Torreón or Monterrey. But relatives there used to like to watch me dance with Tía Lucía and imitate the Everly Brothers and Elvis Presley. Lucía was only about six years older than I was and very, very beautiful. She taught me to dance all kinds of music. I was the only one she was allowed to dance with, and she could not go to dances by herself. We would always dance together. I have no memories of Torreón other than my dad's big house and office building, both in one, on the corner of Morelos and Falcón Streets. Some people lived in the house, sometimes a German man with wife and two daughters, and sometimes a Chinese man and wife and son. I don't remember the names of any of them, except the Chinese boy, Moi Huy. He came to live with us in Crystal City for a few weeks. His father had sent him to the military academy in Castroville, Texas.

The house was a big two-story building, plus basement, with lots of rooms and an open garden in the middle. You could see the sky. The family rooms were in the back end; in the front were several offices. The two German girls were about Tía Lucía's age. I do not know what happened to any of them.

I also traveled as a migrant in search of agricultural work. My dad wanted me to learn how to work at an early age, so he entrusted me to Simón Martínez. I was about ten years old. The Martínez family would go up Texas State Highway 83 all the way up into Wisconsin in a canvas-covered two-and-a-half-ton truck. Many of us would be piled into the back for the three-to-four-day journey. I remember it was hot when we left Texas and cold when we got to

Wisconsin. From the back, you couldn't see anything out the small door that opened for us to get in and out of the truck bed. When they did leave the door open, you just saw the road and road signs from behind. It was like leaving the world behind.

After the other families and individuals in the back of the truck were dropped off at various farms on the way, we would get to Racine, Wisconsin. It would be cold, dreary, and wet in May. We would work in agricultural fields on the Howard Piper farm located on the outskirts of Racine, Wisconsin. Every other weekend, the Martínez family would come together; those that lived in Chicago and those at the Piper farm would alternate weekends. When we went to Chicago, it was a lot of fun. I got to see professional baseball games at Wrigley Field. I learned how big Lake Michigan really was, because it was across the street from the Sheridan School in Racine, where we lived, and it was also in Chicago. And Chicago was the biggest city I'd ever seen, bigger than Milwaukee, Wisconsin.

One time Don Simón and family went to visit a daughter who had become a nun. Her religious order was in Buffalo, New York. We traveled from Racine around Chicago and Lake Michigan into Indiana, across Michigan, Ohio, Pennsylvania and into the state of New York, then up into Niagara Falls. I remember we went to see the falls. It was beautiful. I could not believe such an awesome sight. It reminded me of the little View Masters at Suse Salazar's school where I saw the seven wonders. Niagara Falls was spectacular in sound, sight, and size: tons of water crashing over the side many, many feet below. The roaring sound and the mist is everywhere, so that when the sun hits in just the right spot, you see a rainbow. If you just walk around, you can see many rainbows.

Later, my mother and I, after my dad had passed away in 1957, traveled with Ester Gámez and her son, Jesus, to Gilroy and Watsonville in California. I used to work in the plum and apricot groves and garlic fields. My mom worked at the processing plant, so our shifts didn't coincide. During my freshman year in high school, I actually enrolled in the local school in Gilroy because my mother did not want to return to Texas before the season ended. She was earning good money. When I started spending more time with two local girls, Donna Chappell and Sandy Lymon, and going to rock-and-roll dances, she reconsidered and we returned to Crystal City. I have often wondered what my life would have been like if I would have stayed in Gilroy, California and married Omma or Sandy.

After my father died, my mother and I made less frequent trips to Piedras Negras and the banks. She still went to the *mercado,* but not the banks. She withdrew our accounts and began doing business in San Antonio at the Westside Bank near the *mercado.* My mother introduced me as the "man of the house" to the president there, George Casseb. I felt very grown up and her protector at age thirteen. Mothers have a way of making sons feel real important and proud. I maintained my relationship with Mr. Casseb until he sold the bank.

Later on while in high school, I returned to Wisconsin with some friends, Pete Galván, Jr., Gaspar Méndez, and Joe de Hoyos, for one summer. We went to Wind Lake, Wisconsin, to work on the sod farms. That was an experience. We lived in barracks with about twenty other men. We worked in either irrigation or sod cutting and loading. I tried the cutting and loading but opted for irrigation and even worked weekends on fixing tractor tires and doing general mechanic work. The irrigation crew would work two hours and rest or sleep for three hours, it was 'round the clock work! Most of the time we would go into town in the farm truck and buy beer and something to eat. The sod farm consisted of acres and acres of football-field-like grassy areas separated by trees. We would irrigate some fields while others cut and loaded other fields. The irrigation crews consisted of three men while the cutting and loading crews were made up of six to eight, depending on the size of the tractor and skid. I liked the small crews because we were almost invisible and out of everyone's sight. If we kept up with the irrigation schedule, nobody came to check on us, especially at night.

Local girls would talk to us when we went into town, and we would invite them to party out in the fields. It was like having parties every hour of the day and night.

By the time I had finished high school and started junior college, I did travel more on my own. Right after *Los Cinco* had won the city elections in April 1963, I went to Los Angeles, California, on their behalf to arrange their visit to the West Coast. That's when I met Ed Quevedo of the Mexican American Political Association (MAPA) and other MAPistas. I loved Los Angeles and California. It was lush, green, urban, and teeming with Mexican Americans, like San Antonio, but the weather was cool, not Texas hot. When I returned, I began to plan how I would move to Los Angeles, and I did at the end of the summer of 1963.

When I first arrived in Los Angeles, I lived out of the train station. I kept clothes in a coin locker and used the bathroom to wash up and change. My first job was at the *Los Angeles Times,* delivering advertising copy on a bicycle. As a result, I met people at the gas company and obtained a job referral. The gas company was looking for a printer to run a multilith copier, a small printing press. I claimed to know how to operate that type of machine, but really didn't. When I was offered the job, I immediately went to the city library and read manuals on how these machines worked. I bluffed my way into getting someone there to show me how that machine worked. I learned how to do the jobs myself, always asking for help. During breaks and lunch I would go to the cafeteria or the in-house photography studio.

In the early 1960s, utility companies and other companies hired hundreds of young women to type and handle calls from customers. I made friends with many girls but, on my salary, couldn't afford to go out with them as often as they wanted. Besides, they were looking for husbands and I was not ready for that commitment. To avoid girlfriends with those intentions, I would go visit the in-house photography studio that was run by an old man. He had been there forever. His job was to photograph all the underground grids of any kind below Los Angeles—gas pipelines, electrical lines, sewer and water lines, tunnels—and keep on file the plans for buildings being built, including aerial photographs of the city and the suburbs. He kept all the maps and photos in thin, wide drawers that covered two walls. On another wall he had tables, like architects use, so he could work on the maps and photos. In the center of the room was a huge camera on little railroad tracks. When the camera was at the end of the track, it could photograph a map the size of a large wall, say 20 feet by 12 feet. That is a big map to make into a small picture. He would sometimes show me pictures on the wall of his favorite actress or images he had cut out of *National Geographic* or some other magazine. He eventually let me play with the camera and the files of plans.

When he died no one knew how to operate the camera or work with the maps and photos, except for me. I was the only one who knew where things were. When I spoke up about my knowledge of that operation, I became the head of that one-person department. My salary tripled.

After I had more money than I needed and time to read, I was promoted to department head, I debated on whether to buy a car or continue to ride the bus and enroll in Los Angeles City College to continue my college education. The gas company coworkers encouraged me to finish college. They even offered me release time if my classes conflicted with working hours, provided I did the work later in the evening or on Saturdays. I chose to enroll in college and not buy a car. The process of admission and selecting classes took me an entire day. The college was a huge complex with lots of buildings and full of young people. I was asked for a declaration of a major, if I knew that. I didn't. For years I had said, "Pre-Law," but only as a rote response I had learned since childhood. It did get me to thinking about what I really wanted out of college and life. What was I going to be?

I never made it to classes. Instead, I saved up my money, resigned from the gas company, and returned to Texas to finish college. I came back late in mid-semester of spring, 1964. Classes in Uvalde were almost over and I'd decided I wanted to attend senior college. I applied to Texas A&I University in Kingsville, because some of my friends from Crystal City were enrolled there.

The summer of 1964, Rudy Palomo and I went to Wisconsin in search of work. We teamed up with Juan Patlán and his family, who worked on the flower farms. Rudy and I worked at the flower farm and the Ford Motor Company on a night shift in Waterford, Wisconsin. This town sits on the border of Wisconsin and Illinois. I took on a third job on Saturdays, when I didn't work at the plant, and every Sunday as a lifeguard at the local municipal pool. Rudy and I were the first Mexicans the pool crew had ever met. We became the focus of their attention. They wanted to know why Rudy was dark-skinned and not of African descent. They wanted to know if we were Indians. "What is a Chicano?" they asked. They wanted to know if we really ate hot peppers all the time, even for breakfast. Guys asked us to buy them beer on the Wisconsin side, once they knew we could, even if we were underage.

Rudy stopped coming around the pool when I was on duty, so I became the "Juan and Only" Chicano. When there are few Mexicans in an area, everybody loves you and finds you interesting. When there are lots of Mexicans, everybody blames you for everything that goes wrong and they dislike you. I lived in that area when there were few Mexicans.

Rudy was in love with a girl from back home, Odilia, who's family was in Minnesota working beets. Rudy took off to marry her as soon as he had money saved up. I couldn't afford to live alone and didn't want to. I left my three jobs and joined my mother in Chicago. She was working at a hospital as a nurse's aide. Tía Chelo and Tía Lucía and Tío Salvador and Tío Ignacio also lived there or near there. Tío Ignacio lived in Michigan, but had a place near Indiana on the southern border of Chicago. In Chicago, I got a job with Tía Lucía's husband, Leonard Soderlund, as a mechanic's helper and made enough money to buy a car. When I had saved college money, I left for Kingsville to start senior college at Texas A&I. I graduated in 1966.

After I graduated from my MA at St. Mary's, MAYO members and I traveled to New Mexico to learn about Reies López Tijerina and the Land Recovery Movement. He had an organization of land claimants called La Alianza Federal de Mercedes y Pueblos Libres. *Mercedes* means land grants. All of us had by then read the Treaty of Guadalupe Hidalgo that ended the formal hostilities between Mexico and the United States in 1848. But we did not know the history behind it or what happened after the signing. We wondered why it had the words "Guadalupe Hidalgo" in the title. We found out that these two cities were where the negotiators were located while working on the document. From Reies we learned that the United States had paid Mexico money for some land claims. We also learned that other Mexican lands had been stolen in similar fashion; as those of New Mexico via the Treaty of Velasco. Reies told us we were Indo-Hispanos, the first people made in the Americas. All others, he said, were immigrants, including the Indians who came over the Bering Strait. The Americas belonged to the Indo-Hispanos, the only real native peoples, made here, from here.

We also traveled to Atlanta, Georgia, to meet our black counterparts, the Student Non-Violent Coordinating Committee (SNCC). The meetings between youthful Chicano and black militants were tense. We didn't trust each other; besides, Chicanos were on their turf.

We met Martin Luther King, Jr. in 1967. He was one of the most eloquent and effective speakers I had ever heard. In private, he was very soft-spoken and listened more than he talked. King recognized Reies, not César Chávez, as the leader of the Chicano people. I asked him why and he told me, "Isn't Chávez a union man?" In other words, Tijerina spoke for all Chicanos while Chávez spoke for those in his union. Most black leaders are preachers because part of their mission is to lead. Black preachers minister to the spiritual and material needs of their congregations. Chicanos have no such counterpart. Catholic priests only want to save our souls, not help us with the material and physical demands of living. A few Chicano priests and nuns did join us in civil rights protests and also began to form their own organizations to help the Chicano Movement. In Denver, Colorado, we met Rodolfo "Corky" Gonzales and members of the Crusade for Justice. This was our first experience with non-Spanish-speaking militants proclaiming a mestizo and Aztec origin. We thought that was odd, but it seemed that the further away from the U.S-Mexican border we were, the more Mexican Chicano people wanted to be.

About 1968, I was called up by the military draft. The war in Vietnam was not going well, and more troops were needed. Instead of going into the regular Army, I ended up going to the U.S. Army Reserves and was sent to Ft. Leonard Wood, Missouri, for basic training and to Ft. Sill, Oklahoma, for advanced infantry training. My military service lasted several years, but I had only a few months of active duty. I finished my military service with a rank of E-8, a motor pool sergeant.

When I returned to my former job as investigator for the Mexican American Legal Defense and Education Fund (MALDEF), it was denied to me by Pete Tijerina, the man in charge. Rather than sue MALDEF, I came to an agreement with its lawyer on a severance package. I took the money and traveled with my wife and new baby, Adrian. Together we traveled to New Mexico, Colorado and California to revisit Reies and Corky and to meet for the first time César Chávez and Dolores Huerta. In New Mexico, we got involved in a shootout at a national forest with those opposed to Reies López Tijerina. Tijerina and his followers, including us had occupied Kit Karson National Park re-claiming it as our land. Most of what was once our land located west of the Mississippi River is held by the federal and state governments. Look at a map.

César Chávez had a very integrated operation. He had everything he needed in his forty-acre compound, La Paz, near Keene, California. He had a telephone company, a printing press for his newspaper, *El Malcriado*, a *teatro* to dramatize the plight of farm-workers through one-act plays, a credit union, a health clinic, housing, and lots of volunteers. Dolores was César's right-hand woman. She was a firebrand, full of passion and energy. She is a real superwoman.

When we returned to Crystal City, we wrote a proposal seeking funding for a mobile, migrant Head Start program for infants and children. Basically, we asked for money to care for kids while their parents worked in the agricultural fields. Once funded, my wife and I took off with the migrants to Halstead and Ada, Minnesota, to open a migrant day care and Head Start center. While we were there, every weekend we would drive up into Canada and tour that magnificent open country. We could not believe the temperature and lack of population in Canada and the northern part of the United States. The other phenomenon we discovered was an open border. There was no Border Patrol on the Canadian-U.S. border. No one asked us questions when we crossed into Canada or came back to the United States. It became apparent to us, at that time, that what the United States watches is the Mexican border and Mexicans. Canadians look like white people in the United States. You cannot tell them apart until they talk.

After a month in Minnesota, I got word that my application for the Chicano Studies Graduate Summer Program at Stanford University had been accepted. Overnight, we packed up and drove to northern California. We made tremendous lifelong friends while in that summer program. The professors were fantastic. They taught us from a Chicano perspective. I'd never had that. Octavio Romano, Nicolás Vaca, and others were the first Chicano professors I met on a social basis. I had known some in Texas, but they never drank a beer with me or talked one-on-one with me about everyday things. On weekends, my family and I would go see the sights in San Francisco. We discovered the Mission District, where all kinds of people from Central America lived. I began to like Chinese food. I ate lobster for the first time.

We returned to Crystal City to continue our work organizing the Raza Unida Party. While doing that organizing work, I traveled to many states I had already been to and some new ones. I met Manny Fierro, Betty and Olga Benavides, and Roger Granados in Kansas City, Kansas, and discovered there is another Kansas City, but in Missouri. The two straddle the state border, just like Anthony, Texas, and Anthony, New Mexico, and Little Rock, Arkansas and Texas. The organizing of a national Raza Unida Party also brought me in contact with the Mexican president, Luis Echevarría Álvarez. He took an interest in Chicano politics and our growing numbers in the United States. Leaders in other countries began to take an interest in us, such as Rene Levesque in Canada; Felipe González in Spain; Fidel Castro in Cuba, and Yasser Arafat in Palestine. Many MAYO members traveled to these countries, met with these leaders and discussed the Chicano Movement with them.

In 1975, eighteen members of the Raza Unida Party from various states and I went to Cuba; we went through Mexico. We were invited by the government of Cuba. I had started relations with the Mexican president in 1971 and began traveling regularly to Mexico City. I remember being so disappointed when I landed at the Mexican airport the first time and took a cab into town. The first billboards that were advertising beer had blonde blue-eyed models advertising Mexican beer. Every taxi I rode in seemed to be listening to rock-and-roll music instead of Mexican music. Even at Los Pinos, the official residence of Mexican presidents, the security guards were listening to rock and roll. I didn't understand what was going on.

In 1981, I resigned as county judge for Zavala County, Texas, and left for Oregon. Luz liked Oregon a great deal and it was really beautiful, except when it rained, and it rained more often than not. The Oregon coast near Lincoln City and Newport was particularly beautiful. We went as often as we could to spend weekends on the Oregon coast. You couldn't get in the water; it was too cold.

But the ocean, the waves, the mist, and the sunsets was an extraordinary sight.

While teaching at Western Oregon State University in Monmouth, Oregon, I was selected to be the International Education Director for the state system of higher education. They sent me to Guadalajara, Jalisco, Mexico. When they gave me the check for my expenses, I was smart enough about Mexican politics to know that when there is a change in presidents, there is a change in the dollar-to-peso exchange rate. Usually the peso is devalued in relation to the dollar. I did not cash the check in dollars that was given to me upon departure from Oregon to Mexico because I thought that history would repeat itself when the new president would be elected in July, 1982. Sure enough, the Mexican peso was devalued before the other president was sworn into office in December, so I ended up with a lot of money.

As director of International Education, I chartered buses and took the Oregon students to almost every Mexican state during every vacation break we had. We visited all the resorts, all the major cities, all the archeological zones, all the way down into Chiapas and across to Baja, California. We went everywhere.

Reading and Writing

A passport is required by the State Department of the United States to travel outside of the country. A visa is required by countries you want to visit as a permit to get in. Most of us can't afford that. A U.S. passport costs eighty dollars and a visa costs a little bit, but getting them is time-consuming and complicated. So, a poor person's passport is reading, because if you can read, you can imagine; you can see; you can feel, especially with authors who write well. So, by reading books you can go to Africa, you can go to war, you can fall in love, you can solve a mystery, you can do anything. Reading is a magical experience and Suse Salazar taught me that. My dad taught me how to read *en español,* and my mother taught me how to read in English at home. But Suse Salazar worked it all together and actually got me reading and writing English and Spanish at an early age. I guess that by the time I was four or five, I was able to read and write because of them. They knew that Spanish was going to be subtracted from me in the public school system, and so they added on to me skills in Spanish.

When I hit the public schools, nobody had to tell me; I could see that Spanish-speakers, people like me, were not in the books. All the kids in the early books that I read were Anglo: blonde hair, blue eyes, and with names like Tommy and Jane and Mary. All the songs, rhymes, and children's games came from the Anglo culture. They were all about Anglos and white people. We were not in the books, we were not included in the fun things, we were not in the songs, we were not in the records, we were not in the plays. And when I would go to the movies, they were all in English, except when I went to the segregated Mexican theatres that showed movies from Mexico. In the English-language movies, all the pretty ladies were tall and slender, and blonde, and blue-eyed and beautiful, and they all spoke good English. Even people that spoke funny English, such as British and Australians, were in the movies. Even Indians spoke English, and the actors who played Mexicans in the films also spoke English. Their English was accented or broken, but they spoke it. Mexican characters usually were drunk men with moustaches and bandoliers across their chests. Mexican women were voluptuous and always fell in love with the white guy. So, to children like me these movies were terrible.

Television didn't come into my life until about 1956 when furniture stores in Crystal City started putting black-and-white television sets in their windows. I remember that we would walk over there and crowd the sidewalk, the curb, sitting on the car hoods and even on top of cars, watching the TV inside the window. There was some sound to it, but it was not amplified outside. You had to really strain to listen to what was being said. Later that year, dad bought our first television. It was a Magnavox, snowy, cloudy, and terrible. I soon found out that Mexicans were not on television either. Even Mickey Mouse was Anglo, he spoke English in the cartoons. Popeye and Pluto, too. Everything, everything, everything was in English, all Anglo, nothing Mexican. They had a couple of stereotypical characters, such as Speedy Gonzalez and the drunk mouse.

It was only by reading the Mexican newspapers and magazines that Dad bought or going to Mexican movies or listening to the Mexican radio that I found some sense of identity. I knew there were two worlds, Mexican and Anglo. The Anglo dominated because that's what I had to study, what I had to memorize, what I had to learn. Their history, their stories, their songs, their poems, their rhymes, their actors, their programs, their portrayal of us as drunks and Latin lovers. Thus, public school is not about the 3 Rs. It's about 4 Rs. Reading, Writing, Arithmetic and Racism. Racism is the fourth R. This is how the school maintains a racial dictatorship: showing that only white people are important and the rest are not.

I wondered why we weren't writers, why we weren't actors, and why we weren't the producers. It became clear to me, particularly once I got into politics early on in high school and in my debates. The debate topics were always about important Anglo issues that didn't make any sense to me. But they determined the topics. I remember that I spoke on themes that were dear to them, such as my championship speech on "Democracy on a Penny." I spoke about all the symbols inside a copper penny: *E Pluribus Unum*, Abraham Lincoln, "In God We Trust," and the metal it is made from. I elaborated on every one of those items in my speech. I won the state championship because they just went "ga ga" at the fact that I was praising those concepts, these icons of American democracy. But this is the most undemocratic democratic society there is. It's certainly undemocratic for us Mexicans. It's very democratic for them. I learned that and discussed it in the chapter on politics in this book.

When I began high school and started to read earnestly and diligently, I began connecting the dots. In Texas, all children have to learn about the Alamo in San Antonio. There, according to the Anglos, brave white men were murdered by the evil Mexican dictator, Antonio López de Santa Anna, and his thousands of Mexican soldiers. I made my mother take me down to the J.C. Penney store to buy me a coonskin cap after that school lesson. I wanted to be like Davey Crockett. I didn't want to be like the evil Santa Anna. And in junior high, we revisited that again, and again it got drummed into us that the winners of the Alamo were the Anglo heroes, because they fought for liberty, land and democracy. But that was nonsense. They were thieves. Each one of them wanted to steal Mexican land. They were illegal aliens from Kentucky, Georgia, Tennessee, and other states, every one of them. It was Santa Anna who was coming to carry out the law and, as president of Mexico, to get rid of the invaders, the subversives who had come into Mexico without a passport or visa. They were rabble-rousers. And he did. Later, he was captured when he took a short siesta in San Jacinto. The Tejanos knew that was the Mexican custom after lunch, so they encouraged Sam Houston, who was the biggest coward there ever was, to attack. Sam Houston didn't. It was Tejanos, such as Juan Seguín and others who were with him, that led the attack. They routed the defenseless Mexicans while they were asleep. Conventional European rules of war did not permit such a surprise attack. The soldiers were sleeping in tents. They had their arms quartered outside. They had just eaten. They were not about to fight. European rules stipulated that you told the enemy when and where you would fight, the trumpets would blare and the drums would beat while you would march toward each other and shoot until you ran out of ammo or men. You didn't use guerilla tactics, but Texans did. That is what succeeded in San Jacinto.

I began understanding that. Then I began seeing the dates and the names and the places where the Spanish were and found out that San Miguel de Guadalupe existed before Jamestown in Virginia. Valdez, the city in Alaska, was named after the marine minister from the navy of Spain back in the 1600s. I realized that Santa Fe, New Mexico, is the oldest functioning capital in the United States. And all of these explorations began to make sense to me. Our ancestors were here before Anglos and blacks. Yet, we were quickly dismissed in a paragraph or sentence in a chapter or two of our own history books. We were written off. By the time I hit college, we were a page or two, and we were all portrayed as migrants: farm labor, cheap labor, and agricultural labor. That's the only acknowledgment we received.

In college I began to read books that spoke to me. I remember one of the early books was William Madsen's *Mexican-Americans of South Texas*. The Mexicans in this book didn't even have surnames. It was just Juan and José and María. And it was full of stereotypes. I could not identify with the Mexicans in the book. They were not me. Ruth Tuck wrote a book about Chicano youth and said the biggest problem contributing to Mexican delinquency and crime was their families. We were too many, too poor, too uneducated, and too resigned to fate. That is what she said. I could not believe how these anthropologists could write such things. I had read in other courses the same thing about other peoples. Margaret Mead wrote about Pacific Islanders and John Bingham about the wonders of Machu Pichu in Peru. It was always white people describing what they saw and the way people were. Anglos were always the ones to discover, to find, to know everything, and they wrote books to tell us so. I could not believe them. Why didn't we write books? In the mid-1950s, I watched Charlie McCarthy, the ventriloquist. The Anglo books reminded me of that dummy. There was always some Anglo who talked about us, described us, analyzed us, through his dummy. We did not exist. A dummy spoke for us in books, movies, and television programs. We had to get rid of the dummy so that we could say, "Wait a minute. We have our own voices. We can speak." I started doing that.

I started taking the skills I learned in public speaking and reading to write my own thoughts, Chicano style, and to use my knowledge in politics. And to this day, I can give a good speech with my own voice by speaking for myself. I know U.S. politics and have an understanding of the process. You, too, can write. You can write your ideas and give them to someone else to read. When you write, you feel it. When someone reads your words they also feel, see, and even smell what you feel. The reader gets in sync with the writer. Talking is also powerful. Words are weapons. When you learn that, then you stop being a victim. You become an actor. Otherwise others write about you, they talk about you, and say things about you. You become a victim. It's only when you start writing and you start acting and speaking and taking action that you turn this around. You end the era of the ventriloquist and you find your own voice. Not only in English can you speak, but in Spanish. And you can paint words in people's heads. Those words then become images, and they turn into visions and into the future.

Reading, writing, talking, acting, envisioning, seeing the future. You have to put it down in writing so that it captures the imagination of people. Since the summer of 2003, I have worked with people in organizing Issues Summits. These meetings are one-day gatherings where we discuss problems and seek solutions. We develop an action agenda based on the issues. We have held summits in San Antonio, Houston, San Marcos in Texas, and Kansas City, Kansas. At those events, I usually take the books I have written. I also go to book fairs and other conferences to discuss ideas and sell my books.

My first book was *El Político*. When I was in my master's program, I studied the Mexican American elected official by doing survey research. When I started my Ph.D. program, during my first course I mailed out a questionnaire to six-hundred-and-fifty-nine elected officials with a discernible Spanish surname in Texas. I assumed they were of Mexican ancestry because of their names, but that is not always true. I guess about 25 percent returned the completed survey, and the results of that questionnaire became my first book in which I analyzed who they were and what they were like. Then I wrote *A Gringo Manual on How to Handle Mexicans*. In the 1960s and 1970s, we did not have much political power. We were always being abused by the Anglo power structure. In *Gringo Manual*, I wrote about the inequality of those power relations. Anglos had power and we did not.

My third book was *A War of Words*. I wrote it with Richard Jensen and John Hammerback. It was a book about Chicano rhetoric or speech. I wrote the chapter on "Ondas y Rollos," showing where ideas come from and how they develop into projects. Jensen and Hammerback wrote about the speeches and speechmaking of Chicano leaders. Because it was published only in a hardback edition, it was very expensive. The book was used to teach about Chicanos speaking in public and communicating ideas, using words as weapons and being actors, not victims.

In between books two and three were two small monographs, *Cristal: A Photographic Essay* and *A Diary of the Walkout of 1969*. The former was a collage of photographs identifying key people involved in the civil rights movement in Crystal City, published in 1979, the 10th celebration of the school walkout. The latter was a chronology of events of the December 9, 1969, walkout by students of the Crystal City Independent School District high school.

Book four was *The Making of a Chicano Militant: Lessons from Cristal.* It is my political autobiography of struggle. I tried to focus on the lessons I learned and why I became a Chicano militant during that decade of the Chicano Movement. This book was published by the University of Wisconsin Press and my relationship with the press has proven to be very valuable. Now, other Chicanos publish their books there, such as Armando Navarro who wrote several books on MAYO, the Mexican American Youth Organization, on *The Cristal* experiment, and one on the Raza Unida Party. Ernesto Vigil wrote the book on police surveillance of the Crusade for Justice organization in Denver, Colorado.

My next book came about as a result of a larger project. I wanted to write a book about how the U.S. government spies on its people. The government agencies sometimes also make up lies about people and arrest them under false charges. In 1976, together with others, I began to legally request from the U.S. government the records it has kept on me and other leaders, the Chicano Movement organizations, the La Raza Unida Party, the Mexican American Youth Organization and the Federal Bureau of Investigation's (FBI) role along the U.S.-Mexico border. I have collected thousands of documents from government police agencies. They have been spying on us for years, beginning with Alonso S. Perales and the League of United Latin American Citizens (LULAC) in 1929.

Reies López Tijerina, one of the greatest chicano leaders, is an example of U.S. government spies. Reies published his autobiography in Mexico, *Mi lucha por la tierra.* It was written in Spanish. Most of us do not know how to read in Spanish, so few have read it. I find that most of us did not know of Tijerina nor that he wrote a book. The book in Spanish is five hundred and seventy pages long, hard to find now, practically nonexistent in the United States. In the years that I've spent as a scholar, I have not run across a single book review of this very important autobiography. *They Call Me "King Tiger": My Struggle for the Land and Our Rights* is the title of my English version of Reies' autobiography, which I edited and translated. I decided to do this work for several reasons. First, to introduce Reies to this generation of young people who read English and do not know him. I have found it odd that young people in the United States know a lot more about civil rights leaders such as, Malcolm X and Martin Luther King, Jr. but so little about our leaders. Both of these men are dead, but they have been kept alive in the public arena through books, articles, movies, television shows, celebrations, holidays and even streets and building names. Yet, Reies who is still very much alive, is dead in the public arena. There is no mention of the movement he led and the contributions he made to public discourse. Reies is the creator of the Land Recovery Movement. He introduced us to our birth certificates, that is, the Treaty of Velasco, the Treaty of Guadalupe Hidalgo, and the Laws of the Indies. Reies internationalized the Chicano Movement with his travels to Spain and Mexico and in his attempts to address the United Nations.

While I was at the University of Houston as a Visiting Scholar in 1998-1999, I researched for my next book. The Mexican American Studies program, headed by Dr. Tatcho Mindiola, has a visiting scholar program, a tremendous opportunity for a researcher. The visiting scholar does not teach classes. All that the visiting scholar must do is research and write. I was paid to do what I love! While in Houston, I researched and began to write about Mexican-American public figures in Texas, mostly elected officials. Someday, this book will be published. The book was a long time in the making because the research was based on video interviews I conducted with one hundred and ninety elected and appointed public figures in Texas. These persons were in public office during the years of 1950 to 2003. I've proposed a title: *Liminal Leadership: Mexican-American Public Figures in Texas, 1950–2003.*

Dr. Tatcho Mindiola was among those active with the Chicano Movement, particularly the Raza Unida Party. In fact, he was the leader of the Raza Unida Party organization in Harris (Houston) County, Texas. In that capacity, he hosted one of the many statewide political party conferences we had during the 1970s.

Tatcho rose through the academic ranks to become the director of the Mexican American Studies program at the university.

My fifth book is a republication, a new and revised English-only version of *A Gringo Manual on How to Handle Mexicans*. Sometimes a book gets published and republished with some new material added. In this case, Nicolás Kanellos, Director of Arte Público Press, liked the first book. He wanted more. This book has the same title and content as the earlier version, but contains a hundred new "tricks" that I've added to flesh out the book. It is entirely in English. When Dr. Kanellos and I discussed this project, I also obtained an additional contract to write the sequel entitled *A Chicano Manual on How to Handle Gringos*. Both books, *Chicano Manual* and *Gringo Manual,* are about power. *Gringo Manual* is about power relationships between Anglos, bad Anglos, aka, *gringos* and us, persons of Mexican ancestry in the United States. The stories are about how a powerless group can avoid losing in situations involving powerful *gringos*. *Gringo Manual* is about the beginning of having a semblance of political power in the 1990s and the early years of the twenty-first century. We are now the ones getting and holding positions of power with which to do good. Some of us, however, are as bad as some Anglos, so we can also be *gringos* when we do bad things to people or when we do things for ourselves, pursuing selfish gains and not making the world a better place.

The sequel, *A Chicano Manual on How to Handle Gringos,* is the opposite of *Gringo Manual*. The first one was about powerlessness; this one is about power. In this book, I list the three paths out of power. Actually I posed the paths in the form of questions. Answer the three questions and powerlessness disappears and power arrives. The questions are: How does the world work? How do I make the world work for me? And how do I make the world? The last one is my world, the realm of the activist militant actor, not the victim. We are the kind of people who change the world because of action, ideas, and political courage.

Then I wrote a book about Chicanas. It is titled *Chicanas in Charge: Texas Women in the Public Arena* and I wrote it with Michelle Meléndrez and Sonia Noyola. Michelle is in Albuquerque and Sonia is in Houston pursuing a doctoral degree at Rice University. Altamira Press, a subdivision of Rowman and Littlefield is publishing this book.

The book is about powerful Chicana leaders in Texas during the twentieth century. Within the family and at home, in the community, in political campaigns, on the job and in church, women do all the work and they never get the credit. Women are going to take over the leadership roles in our society in two decades or so. They are going to be our leaders when today's young people have kids in high school. This role change from male to female leadership is going to be very important. Men are not ready to follow women. Women have to undo all the problems that men have created for the last several thousands of years. I don't know if women can change society and us men very quickly. I don't know because I have seen that the first Mexican American who wins public office can not fix everything overnight. Our society has developed over hundreds of years. As Mexicans, we have suffered centuries of mistreatment. Women are going to have a difficult time. They are going to need our help.

* * *

You need to learn how to read and write well. Everyone has a story to tell, and words are weapons. If you can produce a book, you are providing a poor person with a passport to travel into your own mind, through your own eyes, to visit places they can only imagine. That is quite powerful.

Migrants and Immigrants

I read in my junior high history class that the Americas, North, Central, and South, were immigrant nations. The anthropologists and archeologists quoted in my seventh grade textbook said that civilizations have been in the Americas for tens of thousands of years.

I'd always wanted to know who was in the United States first. I asked that question in school. I also asked my dad during one of the many discussions we had at night while sitting outside in our yard. He basically told me that no one really knew. He said that people all over the world had been fighting over land and resources since time immemorial. He didn't know of a single country that had been born without violence, extreme violence. In the United States, he said that the Spanish had explored all of the Americas before the British. He suggested I read the history books and look at the maps closely for that evidence. He showed me in an English-language encyclopedia that the Spanish named most of the places, rivers, mountains, regions, and cities in the Southwestern United States.

He startled me with all this information. Spanish and Mexican people had been in these lands long before there was a United States. I looked at the maps at school and saw all the Spanish names. I also noticed that a lot of the original Spanish names had been changed to an English translation, such as *Gran Cañón* became Grand Canyon; *Montaña* became Montana, because there is no "ñ" in English; *Río Grande* became the Ree Oh Grand; *juzgado* became "hoosegow" for jail; *la reata* became lariat for rope. Spanish words are pronounced in an Americanized twang so you can hardly recognize the Spanish, such as Pecos, pronounced Pay

Cuz; Amarillo, pronounced Am Murr Rila; Colorado pronounced Ka La Rad Dah; Santa Bárbara pronounced Sana Bar Burr Ah; Yucatán pronounced Yuk A Tan; or Puerto Rico pronounced Port Oh Ree Coh.

In high school, the lesson about "Who was here first?" was repeated again in my history and geography classes. I recall teachers explaining that people came from Asia across the Bering Strait and down into the Americas. These first immigrants established societies and civilizations. Immigrants that came later to the Americas, both Spanish and British, were fleeing persecution: religious, political, and economic. Some of the British people that came had been in prison in England and were released, but only if they settled in what became the states of Georgia and Alabama. Catholics were persecuted and Lord Baltimore brought them to Maryland. Most of the British colonists that came to North America were fleeing hunger and economic problems. When they arrived, they still faced hunger and economic problems. Native people had to feed them and show them how to clear land, plant crops, build shelters, use local foodstuffs. That is what started the Thanksgiving celebration.

Many were political prisoners. Others came because they wanted adventure, riches, land, and promotion. Soldiers wanted war; they cannot make rank during peacetime. Others wanted land to become rich. Land creates wealth and wealth could change the life of their heirs. The soldiers, priests, administrator and adventurers that came to the Americas did not come to work. They came with the idea of making others work for them. These conquerors enslaved the native peoples. When those native people died from the diseases the Europeans brought over and from enslavement itself, Africans were imported as slaves. New laborers were brought to make the conquerors wealthy. Land was not bought from the native peoples; it was taken from them. The native peoples were forced to sign documents accepting those terms or die. These documents were called treaties. My dad had impressed upon me that not one single treaty written by the English or the Spanish had fully enforced its terms. The Spanish and the British destroyed native civilizations.

When I worked at a *bracero* (Mexican guest laborers) labor camp as a young boy, I saw hundreds of Mexican men working in the fields outside of Crystal City. They were brought over from Mexico to harvest the crops for the Del Monte Corporation. The Bracero Program began in 1947 and didn't end until 1964, at least on paper—the recruiting of Mexican labor has continued to this day even without official government authorization. The United States is addicted to cheap Mexican labor.

The Mexican Revolution brought a lot of Mexican people into the United States in the 1900s. Then the Bracero Program brought more Mexicans into the United States from the 1940s to the 1960s. People around us who think they are the ones who own the United States started saying, "Go back to Mexico."

I do not understand why certain people think that they own the United States and that only *they* have a right to be here. We have, as human beings, a right to go anywhere. This is our world. It's our planet. It belongs to all of us. From an airplane you cannot tell one state or country from another. There are no signs. However, people put up signs saying, "Welcome to Texas" or "Entering the United States of America."

I've always wanted to know what is Mexican about me. I have an affinity toward Mexico out of respect for my parents and my grandparents who came from that country. I love Mexico. I am a Mexican. I've always wanted to know more about the country and to feel connected to it. My ancestors came from there and they, too, were told to go back to where they came from many times. I could not believe my classmates and even my teachers would say that to us just because we were Mexicans. If we look at the history of the people saying these things, their parents and grandparents came from another country, too. This is the closing door syndrome. They act as if you can close the door behind yourself and not let anybody else come in the door. But that's not reality. People will go wherever they must to find jobs and take care of themselves and their families. My dad suffered from the "back to Mexico" rhetoric. He could not go back after I was born and he had to keep his promise to care for my mother's family after her dad died. Politics also kept my father from going back. Later he established his medical practice and bought property here in Crystal City, so going back was no longer a possibility.

My grandmother on my mother's side had a similar situation. She was from Mexico and always said she wanted to go back. When she married my grandfather, they started a family and she had seventeen kids. Not all of the children lived, and those that died were buried in various places between San Antonio, Lytle, Crystal City, and even Michigan. When my aunts and uncles married, they had kids and lived elsewhere. Before she knew it, she had ties and roots to places all over the United States. She could not go back to Mexico and forego the possibility of seeing her grandchildren and children grow up. My father and my grandmother got tied and rooted to the Crystal City area and couldn't go back.

It is just not the case that people can go back to where they came from. Their offspring, especially those not born in the old country, develop a sense that they belong in the United States. I think I belong here. I don't have any cravings to live in Mexico. I just want to visit and get to know the place.

This is home. Right here. In our case, as Mexicans, the border came to us. We didn't pursue a U.S. citizenship. The United States pursued our land and took took part of Texas in 1836 and then stole the rest of the Southwest in 1848. Both times it was war against Mexicans by Anglos. So, the border has come to us.

In college I began to read more about immigrants. There were French, Russian, Spanish, Dutch, English, and Portuguese explorers and conquerors. They came and some stayed, particularly the Spanish and the British, who were very violent toward the native peoples. People of diverse backgrounds are always coming to the United States.

When I was in high school, the United States began to bring political refugees from Cuba. When I was in college, the United States brought political refugees from Vietnam. In other wars the United States has been involved in, other refugees are invited to this country, such as Jews, Poles, Columbians, Dominicans, and Panamanians. We have received refugees from every part of Central America, particularly in the 1980s. Every time the U.S. military intervenes in a country this creates refugees. These refugees are displaced people. Basically, people who have sided with the United States against their own can't stay behind, so they are brought to the United States.

People who go around saying "go back to Mexico" or "go back to wherever you came from" fail to understand that they have no right to say this. There's no one with any prior right of ownership of North America. How can any immigrant group claim that North America is theirs? But people do.

In 1972, I had my opportunity as a school board member to speak to President Luis Echevarría Álvarez of Mexico. When I met him, he asked, "What can I do for you? What is the one thing I can do for you?" I told him, "Nothing for me but for Mexicans in the United States, you can give them scholarships to study medicine in Mexican universities. Many are not admitted into U.S. medical schools." He and I started a scholarship program called *Becas Para Aztlán* (Scholarships for Aztlán). People of Mexican ancestry in the United States needed medical doctors. They still do. We were unable to get enough Chicano students into medical schools in the 1970s. We still can't. And, Mexican people do not have enough money to afford medical care in this country. Sometimes they are even refused medical care because they are not citizens of the United States.

All presidents have to be accountable for their people wherever they reside. That is why when I met with the Mexican president I made him accountable for his people living in the United States. I insisted he do things for them. With President Echevarría's help, we recorded movies about Chicanos, developed economic development projects, such as the "Mexico HOY," a cultural program, and created bilingual education materials and libraries with Mexican books in many prisons and schools. President Echevarría donated a language lab to the Crystal City Independent School District so Chicano kids could learn Spanish and other languages. This jumpstarted Chicano Studies programs in Mexican universities.

This relationship with the Mexican president is now the norm for others wanting to become the next Mexican president. In fact, contact with Chicano groups became a requirement of presidential politics in Mexico. Presidential candidates met with Chicanos regularly in the 1970s, 1980s, and 1990s. That still is the case today. Mexican candidates to the presidency come to the border and meet with Chicano groups. And groups of us are invited to meet in Mexico. I have met with every Mexican president from Echevarría to Vicente Fox, except for Ernesto Zedillo. Every Mexican president since Echevarría has invited delegations of Chicano groups to every one of their inaugurations. On the other hand, very, very few Chicanos have ever met with the U.S. president.

The Águila Azteca (Aztec Eagle) award is an important award given to a non-Mexican for service rendered on behalf of Mexicans and Mexico. The first award to a Chicano was during the presidency of Adolfo López Mateos. He gave the medal to Porfirio Salinas, an artist of landscapes, especially blue bonnets. Salinas was a Chicano kid from Bastrop, Texas, who was pushed out of school in the fifth grade. During the Carlos Salinas de Gortari administration, more Águila Azteca awards were given to Chicanos than ever. When Governor Vicente Fox Quesada, the current president of Mexico, was campaigning for office, he came to Dallas often. Dallas has more Mexicans than any other Texas city and has the third largest concentration of Mexicans in the United States behind Los Angeles and Chicago. More than 250,000 Mexicans from the state of Guanajuato live in the North Texas area. Fox was the governor of that state. During a campaign visit to Dallas, he said that he wanted to be president of all Mexicans: eighty million in Mexico and twenty million in the United States. That's a very good intention, but it should be executed.

In the 1990s, I helped organize the Grupo de Apoyo para Inmigrantes Latino Americanos (GAILA Support Group for Latin American Immigrants). We had to do this because many immigrants were being victimized. Since they were not citizens, they were afraid to report problems to the police. Employers would hire them and not pay them. Thieves would take their money. Police would beat them. There are many people who make money off of Mexican labor and they want Mexicans to be here. But they don't want them to stay here.

There are lots of things that Mexico could do to create jobs and keep people at home. Over the years in my meetings with Mexican officials, I have mentioned many projects they could initiate. For example, Mexico sells much of its crude oil to the United States. The United States has plenty of reserves and Mexico doesn't. Mexico turns around and imports gasoline, instead of building more refineries for its own gasoline. The Mexican oil industry flares off natural gas to get to the crude oil instead of using the gas. Mexicans just burn the natural gas into the air. The industry could build an infrastructure of natural gas lines to cities, businesses, and homes instead of relying on portable tanks of butane. Mexico needs electricity along the northern border. Electric plants in the United States need natural gas to run turbines that generate electricity. Why not exchange between countries what the other needs and does not have? Mexican workers in the United States send money home. The last estimate was $14 billion a year. That is the biggest source of income Mexico derives from any single source. Tourism and oil sales are not even that much. Central Americans in the United States also send billions of dollars to their respective countries. Not one of those presidents is accountable. They give lip service to how important their people are here. They come visit and make speeches and take photographs, but they certainly don't provide any of the services they need.

The concerns and affairs of Mexicans in the United States do not warrant a cabinet-level secretary or a special agency from Mexico although in Mexico there is one appointed to just about any department. I think it's because we have not demanded it. But I did. When president Vicente Fox came to Austin, Texas, in November 2003 he toured New Mexico and Texas to meet with their governors and Mexicans living in those states. I was invited to be in the Austin audience, so I prepared a letter for him. The letter stated that we needed to get the Becas Para Aztlán program started again. There are more than 35 million Mexican-origin people in the United States now, 15 million more than when he was running for president. I suggested that he award more Águila Aztecas to Chicanos. We need heroes.

I also asked President Fox to declare Mexican food a national treasure and begin a Grano de Oro (Golden Grain) program that would celebrate Mexican food. Most Americans eat Mexican food. In fact, salsa has now replaced ketchup as the national condiment. Yet, many people still discriminate Mexicans.

There are national television programs with commentators and guests who insist the United States has a right to control which people can come into the country. I agree with safeguards against criminals, drug dealers, fugitives, and the like, but not against the refugees we created. National celebrities, such as Rush Limbaugh, Jared Taylor, and Pat Buchanan, think that the United States should be a white country. I've been on national television debating people for years. Jerry Springer invited me to his program in Chicago to debate white and black nationalists who argued against our right to be here. I debated Bill O'Reilly in New York in August of 2002 on "The Pulse." We faced off one-on-one on the topic of immigration. I insisted we should have an open border and allow employers decide who they want to hire, provided Mexican labor is paid a living wage with benefits. On November 2003, I debated both Pat Buchanan and Jared Taylor on MSNBC's "Scarborough Country." On national television I have reminded both O'Reilly and Buchanan that they are the children of immigrants also. The world is not their planet nor the United States a country for whites only.

Politics

There are two different kinds of politics. One has to do with issues, and the other has to do with votes. I first learned about the latter by being involved in school politics. I don't remember much about my junior high years in terms of running for class president and joining clubs. I'm sure that I did because that's one of the things that we get trained in as students, to vote and to begin to learn Robert's Rules of Order.

In 1961, I became junior class president. In 1962, I was both senior class president and student body president. I had figured out that getting a block of votes together guaranteed a victory. In my case, all I had to do was get the Mexican students and a few Anglos to vote for me.

My high school had flipped in terms of population. In my freshman year in 1958, there were more Anglos than Mexicans. By 1960, there were more Mexicans than Anglos. By this time, I had stopped leaving or coming back late in the semester from migrant work, so I was able to get in on the elections that were held in the spring. From 1962 on, most student body presidents and class presidents were Mexican.

In 1963, adult politics came to Crystal City in a big way. The Political Association of Spanish Speaking Organizations (PASO) and the Teamster's Union, both from San Antonio, were encouraging Chicanos in Crystal City to run for seats on the school board and city council. The Chicano community supported an all-Mexican slate for seats on the city council. We called them *Los Cinco Candidatos*. In order to vote in this city election each voter had to pay a poll tax. A poll tax was a payment of $1.75 by every person that wanted to be eligible to register to vote. Voting was seen as a privilege for those who paid the tax; it was not a right of every citizen. The poll tax was clearly a device to keep poor people from getting involved in electoral politics. I was involved in the effort to elect Los Cinco Candidatos as a fringe supporter and sometimes I gave speeches on their behalf. I delivered many speeches at La Placita in the barrio of México Chico in both Spanish and English. Usually, I would talk about the discrimination that was obvious to all—the unpaved streets, the private country club and golf course, the only park we had in La Placita, no streetlights, no jobs, and evil police. To help the campaign of Los Cinco Candidatos, we helped sell poll taxes, even though I was only eighteen, not old enough to vote. Mexican voters bought more poll taxes than white voters. And, of course, we won.

At the same time, I was running for student body president of Southwest Texas Junior College. I was forced to attend this college because I didn't meet the in-state residence requirements at the University of Texas at Austin. I couldn't afford such a high tuition. I had lost out on a scholarship from the Mexican Chamber of Commerce in Crystal City. Although I didn't win that junior college election, I did get every Chicano student to vote for me. Since there were more Anglo students than Mexicans, they out-voted us.

Once, as I returned from college, Raúl Tapia, a local gasoline station operator, drove up to me as I got off the bus at the Dairy Queen and pointed a gun at me demanding I get in his car. I did. He drove me to his home. At his house was a group of white men, all elected officials, including Mexican American County Commissioner, Jesús Rodríguez, and Texas Ranger Captain, Alfred Y. Allee. I was being kidnapped.

Captain Allee had slapped and kicked me once before after I delivered a speech at La Placita. Fortunately, he did this near my house so my mother came out with a shotgun and demanded he leave me alone. He left and she ordered me inside the house. Amazingly enough, Captain Allee did not shoot. I am sure Captain Allee and local Anglos were angry at me and others for selling poll taxes, for helping Los Cinco Candidatos to get elected, and for publishing a newsletter called "In Fact or Fiction?" that exposed the deals that Anglos had among themselves and with Mexican Americans who sided with them.

The Mexican American who was present when I was kidnapped was Jesús Rodríguez. He was appointed to represent us on the Zavala County Commissioner's Court. He owned a large grocery store in town. The group in Tapia's house was under the direction of Captain Allee, who began questioning me about what training PASO and the Teamster's had given me. He wanted to know how much money I was being paid for my speeches and for campaigning for Los Cinco Candidatos. He asked me if I was a communist. Allee and the local sheriff, Charles Sweeten, placed a tape recorder in front of me, as well as paper and pencil. They wanted me to "confess" that I was a communist, that I was paid, and advised as to what to say and do by the "San Antonio bunch," meaning PASO and the Teamsters. I refused.

I refused because it was not true. None of it was true, and I told them that. I was utterly afraid. I knew they were going to kill me for my political work, but I was wrong. They wanted to scare me and make me quit working for Los Cinco. But, as I sat there I realized that they were the ones who were scared. They knew what was going to change in Crystal City. They could not stop the events and hold off change legally, so they were trying to intimidate people. I was there for hours until they gave up. Raúl Tapia drove me home. He took me to dinner at the Oasis Drive-In. My friends saw me there and were relieved when I smiled at them. Tapia kept praising my boldness and courage. Little did he know that I was neither brave nor courageous, just plain scared. If he had been in the kitchen when they brought the tape recorder, he would have seen me sitting on my hands to keep them from trembling.

After the election victory by Los Cinco, I got a job with the city for the summer as my reward for helping in the election. But over the summer, Los Cinco, now city councilmen, began to quarrel with one another and the city manager, George Ozuna. Ozuna was the first Chicano city manager in Texas. I was disillusioned with

politics as it was unfolding. The press kept calling our elected officials incompetent, backward, corrupt, crooked, and illiterate
because they did not have high school diplomas or prior experience in municipal government. Well, what Chicano did in 1963? I
quit my job and left for Los Angeles at the end of the summer and
before school began. Life in Los Angeles was wonderful to me but
I was restless with myself for not continuing my education. I knew
I had to return to Texas.

When I returned in late January 1964, I attempted to enroll at
Texas A&I University in Kingsville, but the semester was already in
progress. Mrs. Virginia Múzquiz, an active member in PASO who
had supported Los Cinco, was running for state representative for
our area. She was the first person of Mexican ancestry to run for
that office. I helped her campaign. I still could not buy the poll tax
or vote for her, but I did know how to campaign. I drove her around
the cities and counties of the district and helped recruit volunteers
during the campaign. She lost. She knew she was going to lose the
race, but continued the campaign because she wanted to show others how important it was to seek these higher-level positions. She
also wanted to increase voter participation among Chicanos by
having someone like them running for public office.

As soon as I arrived on the Texas A&I campus, I was determined
to put Chicanos in student government, but we didn't have the
numbers. There were 1025 Chicano students out of 5,000. I didn't
run for a position. Instead, I, and others who supported my ideas,
organized some of the Chicano students and formed a PASO student chapter. PASO required its members to be twenty-one years of
age. Most of us were under twenty-one, so that became our issue,
to lower the membership age and form youth chapters across state
colleges and universities. I became the head of campus PASO, and
we traveled to San Antonio to attend the state convention. Our goal
was to get the voting age lowered from twenty-one to eighteen
years of age. We made PASO adults feel guilty. We reminded them
that they always invoked the youth as their future, yet they didn't
trust us with the right to vote. We stressed that we were good

enough to go and be killed in the Vietnam war so the South Vietnamese could vote, yet we were not given that same right. And we reminded PASO members that every time they needed volunteers for campaigns, they called on youth and women for help, but not to vote or lead. We won the fight with votes from women members who supported us wholeheartedly. Women know what it feels to be considered second-class and not given credit for leadership ability. A&I University became the first and only PASO campus chapter in Texas.

I was also involved with the fraternity, Alpha Phi Omega, APO; the Young Democrats and the Newman Club, the Catholic students' organization. There was a specific purpose behind each membership I sought. I joined the Newman Club so we could have a place to meet. I joined the fraternity because it was the only one to admit Chicanos to membership. The Young Democrats were mostly liberal Anglo students. I wanted their help when our candidates ran for campus elections. I even teamed up with the Young Republicans on campus to cosponsor an invitation to the first Republican U.S. Senator from Texas since Reconstruction, John Tower, to speak at a student assembly.

We organized the campus by recruiting the prettiest Chicanas to join us and come to our parties. Everyone used to come to our parties because of that. And the pretty girls came to our parties because we were nice to them and took them dancing. We were not in boyfriend-girlfriend relationships with them, we danced and partied. Invariably, we would talk to them about campus politics and the larger Chicano politics in the state, the Southwest, and the nation. We recruited many of the pretty girls to run for various positions: newspaper editor, Lantana Queen (the big event on campus), and for student government. Students vote for pretty and popular people, not for the most qualified or intelligent ones. Since the elections were based on majority vote, and we did not have a majority of student votes, we changed the student government constitution in various ways. First, we proposed an amendment to the student government constitution allowing greater representation in the student government that would include off-campus student representatives; another pair of representatives for part-time students and older students; and a minority student representative. These became Chicano seats.

We called a campus election to change the method of elections from majority to plurality and to eliminate runoff elections. In this way, we won without being a majority through block voting. In those years, student identification cards did not have our pictures on them. So prior to the election, we would have a party and gather all the student cards we could, and vote them on Election Day. I never got to see if our grand strategy had an impact on college elections, because I graduated and left for law school in Houston. Others in PASO took over and have also taken over the student government since that time.

When I went to the University of Houston's Bates College of Law, I did not have time to form a political group. I was working fulltime and attending school fulltime. There were only three other Chicano law students in my class; all others were mostly Anglo males from East Texas. But when I quit law school after the fall semester and transferred in January 1967 to St. Mary's University in San Antonio, I did join others to form the Mexican-American Youth Organization (MAYO). By that time, PASO had almost folded and the other organizations, such as the League of United Latin American Citizens (LULAC) and the American G.I. Forum, were too conservative. We saw MAYO as an organization of organizers. We planned to organize the Chicano youth of the state and the Southwest. We were going to challenge the *gringo* power structure, once and for all. Our generation was going to change politics forever and take back political control in those areas where we were the majority of the voters. The founders of MAYO were Mario Compeán, Willie Velásquez, Juan Patlán, Ignacio Pérez, and I. MAYO did not have many elected positions, as such, although the other four co-founders selected me as the MAYO chairperson in 1968. I did not finish out my term as chairperson because I was called to military duty in October. The following year, when I returned from my tour with the U.S. Army Reserves, I was appointed the lead organizer for the Winter Garden Project. That project led to the Crystal City walkout of students on December 9, 1969, and a few other student walkouts across the state. Students walked out of classes in order to close down the schools for lack of attendance. That is how we protested and demonstrated our will to improve educational opportunities for Chicanos. If we were not going to get a good education, then no one else would either.

Appointed positions are different from elected positions. An appointed position is being named to a position without an election. Basically, those who know you and work with you nominate you. It is a deal done behind the scenes. My second appointed position was that of Urban Renewal Commisioner in Crystal City.

I ran for the school board in Crystal City in 1970 after the successful Chicano student walkout. And on April 3, I got elected school board trustee, along with two others, Arturo González and Mike Pérez. Within the school board trustees, I got elected as president of the school board and served one three-year term. I was appointed by the city council to serve as Urban Renewal Commissioner from 1971 to 1975. In between all of these elections and appointments, I launched the idea to form our own political party. If Anglos have more than two political parties—Democrats, Republicans, Greens, Reform—we should have a Raza Unida Party in Texas. After our electoral victories in the Winter Garden area of Texas, many other Chicano groups in the state also wanted to form local chapters of the political party. Across the country many states wanted to form their own Raza Unida Party. By 1972, nineteen states, including Washington, D.C., had formed the Raza Unida Party. As the national organizer of the Raza Unida Party, I initiated discussions about forming a united leadership team with three Chicano leaders of the time: César Estrada Chávez, Reies López Tijerina, and Rodolfo "Corky" Gonzales. César agreed that we needed unity and political power, but disagreed with having a new political party. He was committed to the Democratic Party leadership at the national level, who had helped him with his unionization efforts. He pledged, however, to campaign for Raza Unida Party candidates involved in nonpartisan elections. And he did. Chávez came to Texas on our behalf many times. Tijerina was lukewarm to the idea of a Chicano political party. He had formed the People's Constitutional Party in New Mexico himself and ran for governor of the state under that banner. He was disqualified from ballot status because he had been convicted in a case that was on appeal. He did not believe we could accomplish much in the electoral arena but promised to help. Corky was eager to start such a national movement. He had organized his state and had candidates for multiple offices. He also did not believe we could win elective office, given our small number of votes in most states. He believed that the Raza Unida Party could run candidates to get media attention and use that forum to educate *la raza* on issues and to present an alternative to the others seeking public office. Corky also did not believe we should ask for money from foundations and the government to fund our activities, political or otherwise. I disagreed with him completely on that. We were taxpayers and we had a right to that money. More importantly, we were eligible to receive such grants and, if we didn't apply, someone else would get our money.

Over Labor Day weekend in 1972, delegates from the states involved and the District of Columbia met in El Paso, Texas, and Ciudad Juárez, Mexico, for a three-day conference to elect the leaders and form the national political party. I was content with continuing in my organizing role; there were other states where we needed to build support for our political party. I wanted César, Reies, and Corky to be national political leaders.

Reies and Corky had a falling out prior to the convention being called to order. I had to convince Reies to stay and help form the political party. Corky did not want Chávez to be invited because he was a Democrat. I had to challenge Corky for the national position as chairman. The election for chairman was heavily contested between Corky and I, but I beat him. I became the national chair of the Raza Unida Party for a long time. I continued to organize around the country and began to travel outside the United States to represent the Chicano community in international affairs. I also remained very active in politics in Texas.

After my school board term, I also ran for county judge in Zavala County under the Raza Unida Party in 1974. I got elected and became the youngest Chicano county judge ever to this day. I served a four-year term as county judge.

I ran for reelection in 1978. That reelection campaign was extraordinary because I was traveling in Europe and doing consulting work for the U.S. Army. I would campaign through telephone messages. I would call campaign volunteers from Paris, Frankfurt, Rome, and the Vatican with news about what I was doing and who I was meeting with. They would record it. Then, they would play the tapes on KBEN, the local radio station, as news and as campaign advertisements. The most dramatic message I communicated was about Pope Paul. He had died when we were in Germany; I had a confirmed appointment with him. He had been pope for two months. We were in St. Peter's Square when the College of Cardinals announced the election of a new pope. The tape recording was quite dramatic as I stood among thousands of people in Vatican Square reporting on the white smoke coming out of the chimney and the figure appearing in the window. Pope John Paul XXIII was the successor.

As county judge, I governed the county with four county commissioners, each elected from a district within the county. I resigned my county judgeship in 1981 and moved to Oregon. In Oregon, it didn't take me too long to get to know people, and I was appointed executive director of the Oregon Commission on Hispanic Affairs. Another Chicano from Texas, Gilberto Anzaldúa, formerly from Harlingen, had started the commission a decade prior but it had no budget or staff. When Governor Victor Atiyeh, a Republican, appointed me as a commissioner to the Oregon International Trade Commission, I took the opportunity to ask him for an appointment to discuss the future of the Hispanic Commission. He agreed to meet. He and I discussed the sorry state of the Oregon Commission on Hispanic Affairs due to lack of money. I pointed out how important Mexican Americans were to the state of Oregon and the great need for a statewide advocacy and research agency to monitor that growing community. I also suggested he change the nature of the commission from a legislative agency to an executive one under his leadership. He agreed and changed the name to the Governor's Commission on Hispanic Affairs and gave it a small budget and staff. Governor Atiyeh appointed me as executive director of this commission. I served in that capacity for a number of years, plus I continued to serve as commissioner on the one dealing with international trade. Then I ran for state representative in Oregon in 1984, during the Ronald Reagan presidential landslide, and lost. I got more votes than any Democrat in my district because I really worked hard. I knocked on the door of every registered Democrat and Independent in the area and personally asked for his or her vote.

The Oregon economy went into a tailspin and I lost my university teaching job. Once again I thought of obtaining a law degree. I returned to Texas in 1986 and enrolled at Southern Methodist University Law School. As a beginning first-year law student, I decided to run for student representative. I was forty-one, but I ran circles around all of the rich white kids in that election. I was elected to student government. The subsequent year Nelda Sánchez was also elected. I showed the few Chicano law students how to win elections, how to campaign, and how to get votes. It's somewhat easy on a campus if you have a plan and you execute it. I didn't run for student office again because I transferred to the University of Houston Law School. After graduation, I returned to work and live in Oak Cliff, a Dallas neighborhood close to downtown. I got involved with the Mexican American Democrats (MAD) of Texas in the Oak Cliff chapter. I was elected the treasurer for the local group, La Causa MAD, and later for the state organization. In the meantime, Bill Clinton was elected president of the United States in 1992. He appointed Lloyd Bentsen to be Secretary of the Treasury and that vacated the U.S. Senate seat he had held. A special election was called in 1993 to replace the senator. I jumped in the race. In that special election I ran against Kay Bailey Hutchinson, several congressmen and twenty-two others. Several statewide television debates were broadcast between the top candidates. I was one of those because the polls indicated I was the choice of 14 percent of the voters. I came in sixth from the twenty-six who ran.

The statewide race also got me established in Texas once again, because many people had not known I was back from Oregon. I had been gone from 1981 to 1986 and was buried in law studies trying to pass the bar examination until 1989. This was the first time they had heard about my return to Texas.

When I ran for state representative in Oregon, I ran as a Democrat, and when I ran for the U.S. Senate I ran as a Democrat. I was forced to do this because the Raza Unida Party had lost ballot status in Texas and was practically dead everywhere else. I have remained involved with the Democratic Party. In 2000, 2002, and 2004, my wife Gloria and I have been elected delegates to our state senatorial conventions. My wife attended the Democratic National Convention of 2004 in Boston, MA, as a delegate from Texas.

Today, as a professor at the University of Texas-Arlington, I teach students and write books about politics. I have also begun to interview many of our public officials in Texas in order to write their stories. I now have two hundred-plus interviews, sixteen with African American officeholders and 195 Mexican Americans. You can view seventy-seven of these at www.libraries.uta.edu/tejanovoices/

I have no aspiration to run for public office again, but you never know what is going to happen. I might. I love politics.